Chicago

Berlitz Publishing Company, Inc.

Princeton   Mexico City   Dublin   Eschborn   Singapore

Original Text:	Laurie Lico Albanese
Photography:	Jay Fechtman
Cover Photo:	Jay Fechtman
Editor:	Richard Wallis
Photo Editor:	Naomi Zinn
Layout:	Media Content Marketing, Inc.
Cartography:	Ortelius Design

*Although the publisher tries to insure the accuracy of all the infor-
mation in this book, changes are inevitable and errors may result.
The publisher cannot be responsible for any resulting loss, incon-
venience, or injury. If you find an error in this guide, please let the
editors know by writing to Berlitz Publishing Company, 400
Alexander Park, Princeton, NJ 08540-6306.*

ISBN 2-8315-7132-4
First Printing April 1999

Printed in Italy
019/904 NEW

CONTENTS

● A (☞ in the text denotes a highly recommended sight

Chicago

CHICAGO AND
ITS PEOPLE

Chicago is a vibrant city built along the shores of magnificent Lake Michigan and the banks of the powerful Chicago River. Synonymous with so many images and stereotypes—the "Windy City," the "City of the Big Shoulders," the "City that Works," the "Second City"—this stunning metropolis of almost 3 million residents is a melting pot of cultures, architecture, music, and food, with enough to satisfy young and old for a weekend or for a lifetime.

For years, Chicago struggled to shake off its reputation as the domain of gangster Al Capone and the legendary site of his showdown with US federal agent Elliot Ness in the era of the Great Depression. Today the city is known for its musical and theatrical achievements, sporting enthusiasm, shopping opportunities, and a rich diversity of restaurants, museums, and artistic venues.

Say "Chicago" and people will likely think of Michael Jordan and his legendary basketball feats, Oprah Winfrey and her daytime talk-show, or the renowned Chicago Symphony Orchestra and its late conductor Sir George Solti. Blues, jazz, ribs, deep-dish pizza, Wrigley Field baseball, and improvisational comedy are just a handful of the city's treasures linked forever in the minds of those who have enjoyed them here in this Midwestern mecca and those who have been influenced by them throughout the world.

First-time visitors are often stunned to see Chicago's 15 miles (26 km) of bathing beaches on the shores of shimmering Lake Michigan. The lake is indeed a vital part of the culture, history, and daily life of this city—including its weather. The third-largest of North America's five Great Lakes, Lake

A walking tour down State Street will reveal the work of renowned architects — and lesser-known artists as well.

Michigan is part of a remarkable freshwater lake and river system that forms part of the border between the United States and Canada as well as one of the world's largest shipping arteries.

Thanks to careful urban planning, there is no other city in America that has as much shoreline devoted to public parks. When the weather cooperates, bicyclists, pedestrians, and joggers take in the fresh air along Lake Michigan from the city's northernmost residential areas, past Lincoln Park Zoo, to the edge of Navy Pier and Buckingham Fountain. In warm months the lake harbors are filled with boats and the beaches are packed with lively volleyball games and languid sunbathers.

Summer is splendid in Chicago, when thousands of people flock to the music and food festivals in Grant Park downtown. But even winter has its own special magic here, in the city that illuminates more than a million lights during November to herald the holiday season. Midwesterners learn how to dress for the cold at an early age, and almost nothing stops them from making the most of their own winter wonderland, with free outdoor skating rinks in the heart of the city and cross-country ski trails in the many forest preserves that ring the metropolitan area. If you come in the winter months (and that means November through March), be sure to pack extra layers of clothing, and don't forget the long underwear.

Remarkably, this city in the center of the continent is distinctly multicultural, ethnically mixed, and friendly to foreign visitors. While it is not an international port city like New York or London, Chicago has more than 60 foreign consulates, supports four major financial exchanges that influence markets worldwide, and has newsstands that carry a wide selection of foreign-language newspapers and magazines. The folks here are nice, but they're also savvy.

Spread out over 228 square miles (592 square km), Chicago is a city of neighborhoods linked by a system of elevated and subway train lines that converge in the area known as the "Loop." Here, everything begins in the downtown area, radiating north to the suburb of Evanston, south to the University of Chicago and the great old homes that sheltered a flourishing African American community in the 1920s, and west to Oak Park, where architect Frank Lloyd Wright made his headquarters for a decade.

Architecturally exciting, Chicago is the birthplace of the modern building. The city's central commercial district burned to the ground in the Great Chicago Fire of 1871, and an army of young architects and engineers rebuilt it with a passionate vision. Many styles of modern architecture can be seen here, from the bustling downtown business center to the sturdy brick-and-graystone residential areas. Even the untrained eye can appreciate the simple grace of Louis Sullivan's designs coupled with their ornate detailing, or the boldness of Mies van der Rohe's steel-and-glass towers. Take a bus tour or riverboat tour—or simply look up. But don't be lulled into thinking you've seen the city just because you've walked along the lake or figured out exactly what buildings are among the city's architectural highlights.

You can learn all about the Loop, yet know nothing of the fabulous boutiques and Vietnamese restaurants on the North Side. You can spend days browsing galleries in River North and taking in shows in the city's newly revitalized theater district, but never see the funky coffee shops and retro clothing stores in Lake View or the Gothic buildings and internationally renowned bookstores at the University of Chicago's campus on the South Side.

Go to Chicago and not hear blues? You might as well go to Washington, DC, and skip the Lincoln Memorial. The modern blues were practically born here, coming north with African Americans in the first waves of migration in 1915. Today the city's blues spots range from those populated by the chino-

---

Can So Many People Be Wrong?

Millions of people pass through the admission gates at Chicago's most popular destinations every year. Here are some approximate annual attendance figures:

Navy Pier	5,325,000
Lincoln Park Zoo	4,133,000
Art Institute of Chicago	2,366,914
John G. Shedd Aquarium	1,775,765
Museum of Science and Industry	1,760,813
Sears Tower Skydeck	1,363,824
Field Museum of Natural History	1,212,475
Chicago Children's Museum	646,300
Chicago Cultural Center	565,882
Adler Planetarium	458,357
Chicago Symphony Orchestra	453,059

A brief moment of peace: the sun rises on the Chicago River and another busy day in the city.

slacks-and-leather-jacket crowd to smoky rooms presided over by gritty music-makers. You just never know who might show up in Buddy Guy's Legends to play a riff or belt out a classic.

A look at the city and its people would not be complete without mentioning some of the literary greats who have lived here, including novelists Nelson Algren and Saul Bellow, poet Carl Sandburg, the first African American Pulitzer Prize-winning poet Gwendolyn Brooks, and Pulitzer Prize-winning playwright David Mamet. These artists drew upon what is best in the city—its never-quit attitude and its traditional Midwestern values—and churned out great words that endure.

An industrial city that prides itself on a simple work ethic and supports hundreds of international corporations,

Chicago has been the destination for generations of immigrants who have kept it growing. Home to more Polish people than any other city outside of Warsaw, Chicago also has a large and expanding Mexican population, an Asian community that has spread from a small Chinatown to points north and west in the city, and significant groups of Greek, German, Ukrainian, Italian, and Irish residents as well. The city's population is 45 percent African American, the result of two waves of migrations from the rural South.

Culture in all its forms can keep area visitors going for days. The centerpiece of the museum experience in Chicago is the new downtown Museum Campus, which links the natural history museum, aquarium, and planetarium in a park-like setting at the edge of the lake. Many people like to see the main attractions first, then set out for more unique sites that pique their own personal interest. Chicago has an unparalleled museum of

Mexican art, a museum of African American history, a museum of holography, several devoted to architecture, one just for children, and numerous others.

There are more than 45 art museums and countless small galleries in Chicago. The Art Institute of Chicago is known for its impressive collection of famous French Impressionist paintings, and

The lovely views from the river esplanade are well-enjoyed with a friend.

new museums of contemporary and American art offer venues for various modern and postmodern work. Visitors need only tour the city's dozens of public outdoor sculptures, by such stellar artists as Pablo Picasso and Joan Miró, to see that the citizens of this city value and appreciate art.

Lively politics and popular culture, too, are here in abundance. The nickname "Windy City" comes not from Lake Michigan's blustering wind but from the city's blistering politics. If father-and-son mayors Richard J. Daley the elder and Richard M. Daley the younger didn't put this town on the map, then Michael Jordan and the Chicago Bulls' six National Basketball Association championships and talk-show host Oprah Winfrey and her TV and film studios surely have created enduring legends here in America's heartland.

And while visitors enjoy the many cultural, intellectual, and culinary opportunities, shopping is ranked as one of the most popular leisure pursuits. No doubt that is because the shopping is splendid in Chicago, from the star-studded line-up of famous retailers along Michigan Avenue to the countless specialty stores and unique shops in the various neighborhoods that radiate from the Loop.

Nearly 30 million people visit the Chicago area each year. The city's vast conference center hosts conventions, trade shows, and corporate meetings, making it the nation's top city for business. Hotels here are generally expensive but impressive, the public transportation is easy and accessible, and taxicabs can be hailed with a wave of the hand, rain or shine.

You can ride the tour buses, step in and out of taxis, and walk the neighborhoods with a map in your hand. But the people are so friendly, and the lake is so pretty, that Chicago will inevitably lure you to put down your guidebook and simply enjoy the feelings of well-being and adventure it carries on its strong shoulders.

A BRIEF HISTORY

Long before Chicago was the Midwest's primary metropolis, it was the center of activity for furriers and traders. These hearty Frenchmen were drawn to the original settlement of Jean Baptiste Point du Sable, the French-speaking black man who built the first cabin on the north bank of the Chicago River in the late 1700s. Du Sable's settlement became a linchpin in France's hold over the territory, which was a major passageway between the Mississippi River and the Great Lakes.

Even after the American War of Independence, France and Britain continued to vie with the US for control of the strategic location at the mouth of the Chicago River. It was here in 1803 that the Americans built Fort Dearborn to help the government assert dominance over the area. Today the stunning Wrigley Building, the gothic Chicago Tribune Tower, and

Michigan Avenue Bridge now stands where Fort Dearborn once protected the mouth of the Chicago River.

busy Michigan Avenue Bridge converge where the old fort stood, near the swells of great Lake Michigan.

Fort Dearborn was under the command of Captain John Whistler, grandfather of the famous American painter, James McNeill Whistler. The fort became a center of economic activity, peopled by a lively mix of Americans, British, Scots, and French-Indians in a soon-to-be-city that would retain the richness of ethnic diversity throughout its years of spectacular growth. The fort was destroyed by Native Americans in 1812 and subsequently rebuilt in 1816.

Native Americans resisted the Europeans' usurping of the land around Fort Dearborn, but resistance ended with the defeat of the Chief Black Hawk, chief of the Sac tribe, in 1832. The US government forced the American Indians to sell their lands for a fraction of their worth, and the Native Americans were moved west. It is said that Chicago derives its name from a Native American word for "wild onion," referring to a weed that once grew abundantly in the marshlands and riverbanks here.

Chicago was incorporated as a city in 1837. Its population was just a little over 4,000, but the number of inhabitants grew exponentially over the next twenty years, exceeding 300,000 people by 1861.

Railroads, Steel Mills, and Slaughterhouses

The railroad came to Chicago in 1848, the same year in which the Illinois and Michigan Canal permanently linked the Mississippi River to Lake Michigan via the Illinois River. Midwestern farmers were able to process and ship their grain and livestock through Chicago, and Chicago inventor Cyrus McCormick built the first reaper, which later filled in for farmhands during the years of the American Civil War and helped the McCormick family amass a fortune. The first official American commodity exchange, the Chicago Board of Trade, also was established in

1848. With all these events, the city's reputation as a hardworking "City of the Big Shoulders" was born.

The Illinois and Michigan Canal (dug by Irish laborers) brought ships from the Caribbean to New York up the Mississippi River and through the Great Lakes area, helping the entire state of Illinois prosper. But it was the Illinois Central Railroad —built on land relinquished by the city in the first national land grant—which grew most phenomenally in response to the thriving economy and increasing demand for rapid transportation. Chicago soon was a railway hub, moving logs from Michigan, coal from the south, iron ore from Minnesota, and wheat, corn and cattle from the prairie, and attracting thousands of immigrant workers to stand on its big shoulders.

Lake Street, which now runs through the Loop, was the center for both residential and commercial activity during the

city's early days as a thriving metropolis. Chicago's most important businesses were housed in brightly colored, Italianate-style buildings surrounded by gracious homes. The poor lived close by, mainly because land transportation was still difficult. Irish, German, and Scandinavian immigrants were already here in droves, living in shantytowns and tenements near the river.

The old Water Tower: one of two downtown buildings spared in the great fire.

The city's first steel mill was built in 1857, and the Union Stock Yard, the livestock slaughterhouse immortalized by writer Upton Sinclair in his grim and gritty novel *The Jungle*, opened on the South Side in 1865. The stockyards became the major suppliers of meat to the nation and were both a blessing and a scourge upon the city. Waste from the stockyards flowing from the Chicago River polluted Lake Michigan so badly that reversal of the river flow (away from the lake) eventually became necessary as a last-resort health measure. But this wasn't done until thousands of people had already died in epidemics of cholera and other pollution-related diseases.

The Great Chicago Fire

Legend has it that Mrs. O'Leary's cow kicked over a bucket in her near South Side barn and started the infamous Chicago fire of 1871. The fire burned for almost two days, covering the central portion of the city and destroying most of it. First the wooden houses in the Irish "Patch" southwest of downtown and then the downtown buildings themselves went up in flames. When the roaring fire was finally checked by rain, more than 1,600 acres (650 hectares) of the city lay in ashes, from the near West Side, across downtown to the lakefront, and as far north as Fullerton Avenue.

The fire seemed to mark the end of Chicago, but there were some blessings. Miraculously, only 300 people lost their lives in the devastation. Industry, much of which had already moved to the outskirts of the city, had been spared. The Union Stock Yard, by then a vital part of the Midwest's economy, continued unharmed. Insurance money poured into the city, and Chicago rose like a phoenix from the ashes.

Visitors today often hurry past the old Water Tower and Water Pumping Station on North Michigan Avenue without realizing their significance. These two yellow limestone buildings were the only structures spared in downtown Chicago. Everything around them was destroyed—except for the city's spirit.

Within weeks, the city's leaders had taken control of reconstruction. There were 90,000 people left homeless from the fire, and rebuilding needed to begin quickly. The city council forbade construction of any wooden structures downtown, ensuring that the buildings erected in the area after the fire would last into the next century and beyond. But the council's decision also forced the city's many working poor to move even farther from the central business district in order to find the cheaper wooden housing they needed.

The commercial heart of Chicago was reconstructed, predominantly with cast-iron structures like the Page Brothers building, which is still standing on the southeast corner of State and Lake streets. Two years after the fire, the city's downtown business and financial center was back in full swing. By 1885, Chicago's architectural leadership was established when the world's first skyscraper, the nine-story Home Insurance Company building, was erected downtown. The city built the first elevated trains in 1892 and hosted the Columbian World Exposition in 1893, commemorating the 400th anniversary of the discovery of North America.

The Rise of the Labor Movement

As a new economy rose from the ashes of the fire, unrest also grew. Perhaps clashes between the working poor and the industrialists were inevitable in a city with so much industry and so many immigrant laborers. Late 19th-century Chicago saw several such clashes. Hungry workers marched on City Hall in 1873, and in 1876 workers at Chicago's largest factory, McCormick Reaper Works, went on strike. The infamous Haymarket Square riot of 1886 involved some 60,000 laborers demanding an 8-hour workday: workers clashed with police, resulting in nine people being killed and 150 wounded.

Pullman Company workers went on strike in 1894 after the corporation that built railway sleeper cars—and provided housing to its workers—reduced wages without reducing rents. The American Railway Union responded with a sympathy strike, uniting black and white laborers for the first time; it raged for more than two weeks and was a major turning point in the US labor movement. The Industrial Workers of the World (the "Wobblies") was formed in Chicago in 1905.

This likeness of General Ulysses S. Grant stands in Lincoln Park.

By 1890, the city's population had surpassed one million. Immigrant workers from as far afield as Poland, Serbia, Russia, Czechoslovakia, Lithuania, Italy, and Greece had shown the City of Big Shoulders just how big their own shoulders were, and just how much they would take before shrugging off some of the heavy burden.

The Chicago School of Architecture

The aftermath of the Chicago Fire brought architects from around the world to the city in the center of the North American continent. They were led by architect-engineer William Le Baron Jenney, who had built the Home Insurance Company building using an all-metal skeleton of cast-iron columns and beams, creating a prototype for future skyscraper design. Spurred by the building boom, architects from around the world poured into the city, creating a legacy that endures today as the "Chicago School of Architecture." Louis Sullivan, Daniel Burnham, Martin Roche, and William Holabird worked for Jenney and emerged as leaders of the school's style of architecture. In fact, Burnham so pleased city leaders with his design for the 1893 Columbian Exposition (which included the building that now houses the Museum of Science and Industry in Hyde Park) that he was hired to create a master plan for Chicago's expansion into the 20th century. "Make no little plans," Burnham wrote in his famous *Plan of Chicago* (1909). "Make big plans; aim high in hope and work." Burnham was instrumental in building an infinitely navigable city that preserved its waterfront with parklands. Today, visitors to Lincoln Park, Grant Park, and the new Museum Campus can thank Daniel Burnham for his foresight.

The Chicago School was built around the now-famous maxim "form follows function," and the buildings from this era are often an interesting mixture of simple economy of space and extravagant appointments. Sullivan's most famous surviving building, the Carson, Pirie, Scott store (1904) on State Street, features simple steel walls complimented by a series of richly ornamented metal panels adorning the entranceway.

It was Sullivan who had made the famous pronouncement about form and function, but it was his protégé, Frank Lloyd Wright, who carried this decree to its ultimate level of architectural triumph. Wright believed environment should determine a building's form, and so the Prairie Style was born in the flat heartland of America. Wright's distinct design style —characterized by sleek buildings constructed with materials selected for their natural colors and textures, combined with interiors that give a sense of spaciousness by flowing

Robie House was designed in 1909 by Frank Lloyd Wright, leading figure in the Prairie School of architecture.

from one room into the other—can be seen at the Robie House in Hyde Park, and in the Oak Park neighborhood where the architect lived from 1890 to 1910.

Many great works from this exciting period of architectural discovery and experiment survive today, most notably Burnham and John Wellborn Root's Rookery Building (1888); Holabird and Roche's Pontiac Building (1891); the Auditorium Theater Building (1889), which was designed by Sullivan together with Dankmar Adler; and the Chicago Board of Trade (1930), designed by Holabird and Root as a soaring golden monument to the graceful Art Deco style.

These ornate structures from the early days of Chicago's architectural grandeur are no less stunning when seen beside those monuments to minimalism built by such latter-day greats as Ludwig Mies van der Rohe, modernist Helmut

Jahn, and structural engineer Fazlur Khan, whose cross-brace design was employed to build the John Hancock Center (1969) and the even-taller Sears Tower (1974).

Gangsters and Politicians

Corruption was long associated with Chicago politics and its people, and with good reason. First it was the corrupt leadership of Mayor William Hale Thompson in the 1920s; then it was the machine politics of Mayor Ed Kelly and local Democratic Party boss Pat Nash, who ran Chicago politics for 50 years on a system of dirty paybacks and green payoffs. Democratic Mayor Richard J. Daley led the city from 1955 to 1976 on a similar crony system, rewarding friends with jobs and with money for pet projects in their neighborhoods.

Evidence of local power gone awry reached its height in August 1968, when some 16,000 Chicago police officers waged what investigators later termed a "police riot": beating anti-Vietnam War protesters during the 1968 Democratic Party Convention, riding on motorcycles over the bodies of injured peaceniks and even sidewalk bystanders, and storming the hotel suite of presidential candidate Eugene McCarthy. The police were defended on television the next day by a wildly gesticulating Mayor Daley—a move that further tarnished the Democratic Party and Chicago leaders for decades.

With so much palm-greasing and backstabbing in Chicago's political legacy, it's no wonder the city was headquarters for the nation's most notorious gangsters during the Prohibition Era (from 1919 to 1933), when an amendment to the US Constitution severely restricted the sale and use of alcoholic beverages. Most infamous of all the nation's gangsters was Al Capone. This Italian mob boss led his underground kingdom of whiskey-running, prostitution, and gambling from his South Side home from 1924 to 1931. He bribed Chicago police officers and killed off his rivals in minibattles that culminated in the 1929 St. Valentine's Day Massacre on North Clark Street, when seven members of the Bugs Moran gang were gunned down by Capone's mobsters, who were disguised as policemen. Federal agent Elliot Ness and his task force of men known as "the untouchables" (because they couldn't be bribed) finally arrested Capone in 1931 on the unglamorous charge of tax evasion, and the city put the worst of its gangland history behind bars.

As for corrupt politics, the powerful Chicago machine seems to have faded into the past, despite the election of Major Richard M. Daley (son of Richard J. Daley) to the office in 1989. Mayor Daley the younger has been begrudgingly praised by friends and foes alike for his fairness and for efforts to bridge the racial gaps and ethnic tensions that have long polarized the city.

Black Chicago

A large portion of the city falls into the area known as the South Side, a sprawling network of neighborhoods rich in history and often overlooked by visitors. It became a center of African American life during World War I, when thousands of black workers and their families migrated here from the rural American South, lured by the promise of plentiful jobs, honest labor, and a home to call their own. They settled largely on the South Side, creating a flourishing center of arts and culture that coincided with the Harlem Renaissance in New York City.

Chicago became the nation's jazz leader in the 1920s, when music poured into the streets from clubs along State Street on the half-mile strip known as "the Stroll." These clubs showcased such performers as Jelly Roll Morton and Louis Armstrong, and were predecessors to the South Side blues clubs of the 1930s and 1940s that gave rise to such enduring artists as Muddy Waters and Otis Spann.

The city's black population more than doubled in a decade, exceeding 100,000 by 1920. In a city known for its segregation and purported racial intolerance, it's no surprise that the tensions that rippled across the country during these years of African American migration also prompted the Chicago Race Riot of 1919. It began in the all-white section of the South Side known as Bridgeport (home of Mayor Richard J. Daley and birthplace of his son, Mayor Richard M. Daley); it took 13 days, and dozens of deaths, before the riots were quieted.

Chicago's second great African American migration began in 1941. A look at the disastrous Robert Taylor and Cabrini-Green public housing projects, built in the 1950s and 1960s, turns a grim spotlight on the lives of Chicago's poor blacks, many of whom came looking for opportunity and found discrimination instead.

In 1983 the city elected its first African American mayor, Harold Washington, and in 1993 Illinois sent the first female US senator of African American descent—Chicago politician Carol Moseley-Braun—to Washington, DC.

The city's most visible superstars currently are African Americans, whose careers and exemplary management of their success make them role models for young people around the world. Talk-show host Oprah Winfrey has her multimillion-dollar film and TV complex, Harpo Studios, in the West Loop. And Michael Jordan, the retired Chicago Bulls basketball star, still makes his home in a Chicago suburb. Arguably the greatest basketball player of all time, Jordan led the Bulls to their six National Basketball Association championships in 1991, 1992, 1993, 1996, 1997, and 1998. Outside the team's new stadium, United Center, an enormous statue of a soaring Jordan stands as acknowledgment of the recognition he has brought to the team and to the city.

Chicago Today

Downtown Chicago's future looked bleak in the 1960s. Like other urban areas, the Windy City faced suburban flight, waning industry, and racial tensions. But a development boom has transformed what was a decaying central core into a vibrant economic and cultural hub. Some of the world's tallest buildings put a thoroughly modern face on the city's continued transformation. The $10 billion construction frenzy in the 1980s that revitalized the city's downtown university campuses continues today with the re-emergence of State Street as a shopping and theater magnet. The Union Stock Yard is now an industrial park where 8,000 people are employed at some 90 firms. And urban pioneers who rehabilitated Old Town and Lincoln Park houses some 30 years ago can now sell their homes for ten times what they paid for them; this "gentrification" has spread to the neighborhoods of Wicker Park and Bucktown.

With a population that is proud of the city's history, heritage, creativity, and practicality, Chicago is poised for growth well into the 21st century.

A hero for the present: this statue of Michael Jordan graces United Center.

Historical Landmarks

1779   Jean Baptiste Point du Sable, a French-speaking African American, starts first permanent settlement on the north bank of the Chicago River.

1803   Americans build Fort Dearborn at mouth of Chicago River.

1837   Chicago incorporated as a city of 4,000 residents.

1848   The railroad comes to Chicago; Illinois and Michigan Canal links the Mississippi River to Lake Michigan via the Illinois River; Chicago Board of Trade established.

1865   The Union Stock Yard opens on Chicago's South Side.

1871   Much of the commercial center of the city is destroyed by the Great Chicago Fire; Water Tower and Pumping Station left standing on Michigan Avenue.

1885   Construction of the Home Insurance Building, at nine stories the world's first "skyscraper."

1886   Haymarket Square labor demonstrations for an 8-hour workday lead to riots in which nine people die.

1893   The Columbian World Exposition leaves such landmark structures as the Museum of Science and Industry and the Ferris wheel now at Navy Pier.

1919   Chicago "Race Riot" lasts 13 days.

1929   "St. Valentine's Day Massacre" on North Clark Street, involving members of the Al Capone and Bugs Moran gangs of mobsters.

1931   Jane Addams wins Nobel Peace Prize for her work in public education and child welfare.

1941   Start of the second great wave of African American migration to Chicago from the US South.

1942   Enrico Fermi and team create the world's first self-sustaining nuclear chain reaction at University of Chicago.

1968   Demonstrators at Democratic National Convention are beaten in what is later officially called a "police riot."

1973   Sears Tower becomes the world's tallest building.

1983   Harold Washington elected as Chicago's first African American mayor.

1996   State Street Revitalization Project restores luster to the Loop.

1998   The Chicago Bulls basketball team, led by Michael Jordan, win their sixth NBA championship.

WHERE TO GO

There's so much variety in Chicago—where to go depends upon what you enjoy. First-time visitors often want to see the city's Loop and Michigan Avenue highlights, then perhaps venture to a few offbeat locations in the outlying areas such as funky Wicker Park, Wrigley Field for an afternoon baseball game, or the architecturally beautiful suburb of Oak Park.

A good measure of any city's offerings are those frequented by the locals. Chicagoans' own favorite cultural destinations include Navy Pier (home to a Ferris wheel, indoor carousel, and the Chicago Children's Museum), Lincoln Park Zoo, the Art Institute of Chicago, Shedd Aquarium, the Museum of Science and Industry, Sears Tower Skydeck, the Field Museum, and Adler Planetarium.

On St. Patrick's Day, the river is colored green (don't worry, it doesn't hurt the fish!) and green bagels and green beer are served in local eateries as a few million people gather to see the parade through the Loop.

Weather also will dictate your wanderings. Brutal snow or freezing rain whipping off Lake Michigan can discourage all but the most hardy from shopping and sightseeing along Michigan Avenue or State Street, while warm weather will inevitably beckon you to the lakeshore and the newly updated (to the tune of $110 million) Museum Campus.

While the city has more than 80 distinct neighborhoods, it's easiest to think of the broad metropolis in terms of the Chicago River, which branches from the lake in the shape of a "Y" that divides the city into three basic areas: North Side, South Side, and West Side (there's no "East Side"—unless you're boating in Lake Michigan). At the middle of the "Y" is the Loop, Chicago's central downtown district.

Finding your way around the city is easy once you understand the basic system that organizes streets and building numbers. From one end of the city to the other, all street numbers advance along a simple grid, with "zero" at the corner of Madison and State streets in the Loop. Along every street to the north, south, east, and west of this corner, the addresses increase in equal increments (usually 50 or 100 per block). Chicago Avenue, for example, is known as "800 North"; Division Street—the next major artery to the north—marks addresses as "1200 North." It's not unusual to hear people get into a taxicab and say, "We're going to 2000 North and 800 West," which would put them right at the corner of Halsted Street (800 West) and Armitage Avenue (2000 North).

DOWNTOWN CHICAGO

Chicago's downtown area is its heart. Here is the commercial and cultural nerve center of metropolitan Chicagoland

Wherever you want to go in Chicago, the "El" and other public transportation will get you there.

—and its transportation hub—along with top museums, galleries, theaters, department stores, and exclusive shops, as well as some of the most fashionable addresses in town. Although it was destroyed more than 125 years ago by the fire, downtown was quickly resurrected with a vibrant new spirit and modern construction that showed the world how business and culture could thrive together. Arrayed like jewels along the shores of Lake Michigan are a lineup of treasures: from the Museum Campus at the south end of Grant Park to the Magnificent Mile and the Gold Coast a few miles north. It is here in downtown Chicago that the picture on your favorite postcard was probably photographed.

In and Around the Loop

Everything begins in **the Loop**, the downtown district where the city's elevated train lines (the "El") converge to form an actual "loop" around an 8-block area. While this small, dense area defines the Loop proper, its boundaries have expanded to include much of the downtown business area. The historic center of Chicago, the Loop is an energetic place during working hours. Thanks to millions of dollars pumped into urban revitalization programs, it is beginning to experience a night-life resurgence city fathers have been desperately seeking for almost two decades.

The Loop encompasses City Hall and the Richard J. Daley Center, the original Marshall Field's and Carson, Pirie, Scott department stores on State Street, the city's financial corridor, and the newly revitalized downtown theater district. Outside the Loop proper but still within its bustling influence, you'll find Orchestra Hall, the Chicago Cultural Center, the new Harold Washington Library, and the Art Institute of Chicago.

Just for fun, on Saturdays from June through October you can take a guided tour of the Loop on the elevated train, sponsored by the Chicago Transit Authority (CTA) and narrated by Chicago Architecture Foundation guides. Tickets and information on the 40-minute tour are available at the Chicago Cultural Center (see below).

Chicago's Jewels on Michigan Avenue

The **Chicago Cultural Center** (which stretches along the west side of Michigan Avenue between Randolph and Washington streets) is in fact the most natural place to begin exploring this part of the city. More than one million people each year visit this imposing building for its many resources and attractions. Built as Chicago's central library in 1897, this Neo-Classical landmark now houses the city's main tourist information facility at its Washington Street entrance. Information on Chicago past and present is abundant in this room. Take time to talk to one of the well-informed visitor's center guides, but don't end your visit there. Stop for a cup of coffee in the lobby café, browse through various changing exhibitions, then take one of two grand staircases from the main floor and gaze up at the world's largest (38 ft/11½ meters tall) Tiffany dome on the third floor. The **Museum of Broadcast Communications**, a small but modern museum dedicated to TV and radio, is also housed in the Cultural Center, near the Washington Street entrance. The Radio Hall of Fame and a few hands-on exhibits make this a fun and nostalgic quick-stop on your swing through the Loop.

Of course, for the best art display in town you won't want to miss the **Art Institute of Chicago**. Heralded by a pair of majestic bronze lions adorning the front staircase on Michigan Avenue (at the foot of Adams Street), this 107-year-old institution houses the most impressive French Impressionist collection this side of Paris, and has in its permanent collection notable pieces by Monet, Renoir, van Gogh, Degas, Cézanne, and others. Among the most famous works in the museum's diverse collection, spanning 5,000 years of art history, are George Seurat's *A Sunday on La Grande Jatte,* Vincent van Gogh's *Self-Portrait*, Grant Wood's *American Gothic*, Edward Hopper's *Nighthawks*, Mary Cassatt's intimate moment in *The Bath*, and the largest painting ever done by Georgia O'Keeffe, *Sky Above Clouds IV*. The museum also hosts traveling exhibits of international renown.

The Art Institute of Chicago houses a large, varied collection spanning 5,000 years.

Regular visitors to the Art Institute always enthuse about the spectacular Thorne Miniature Rooms, a lavishly detailed diorama-like series of 68 small rooms showing centuries of interior design. The first-floor Japanese Meditation Room is a wonderfully dark and quiet place to soothe your mind. The photography gallery displays temporary shows, rich in their diversity and often impressive. Downstairs, the Kraft Education Center has a magnificent reading room and hands-on exhibit spaces for young people. In summer months, have a salad in the outdoor Garden Café and relax.

Across from the art museum, at 220 South Michigan Avenue, you'll find **Orchestra Hall**, recently reopened after a 3-year restoration and expansion that included acoustical

Constructed by popular demand—the design of the Harold Washington Library Center building was put to a vote.

renovations plus the addition of a first-class restaurant and an interactive music learning center dubbed "ECHO." Home of the **Chicago Symphony Orchestra**, founded in 1891, Orchestra Hall is an architectural landmark where classical, jazz, pop, world music, and other performances can be heard most evenings and weekend afternoons.

It's not far south from Orchestra Hall, just a few blocks, to the new main branch of the city's library system, the **Harold Washington Library Center**, which occupies an entire city block bounded by State Street, Van Buren Street, Congress Parkway, and Plymouth Court. This is Chicago's nine-story Beaux Arts-style monument to its citizens' continued good taste in architecture (it was built in 1991 according to a design chosen by public vote) and high regard for the free institution of the pubic library. In addition to a sizable book and newspaper collection (including foreign-language newspapers from around the world on the fourth floor), there is also a spacious second-floor children's section, sections devoted to Chicago authors and to Chicago architecture, and a winter garden atrium on the top floor.

State Street

Fresh from your moments—or hours—spent inside with history and art, you can shop along State Street and take in the newly renovated streetscape. Green kiosks put up by the city mark the area's architectural highlights, past and present. Follow the self-guided walking tour to see some of Chicago's splendid architectural achievements, including the great department stores: **Carson, Pirie, Scott** (1 South State) and **Marshall Field's** (111 North State). Be sure to look up at the entrance to the Carson building for the famous iron grillwork that was part of Louis Sullivan's landmark design. Then stop for lunch in one of Marshall Field's newly-remodeled seventh-floor eateries: during the winter holidays you might want to take someone special to the Walnut Room, or have hot cocoa and cake at the foot of Field's spectacular Christmas tree.

> In inclement weather, duck into the interconnected underground walkway at City Hall, the Daley Center, Marshall Field's department store on State Street, or the Chicago Cultural Center. It connects "El" stations, too.

The central Loop area has been experiencing a resurgence lately, thanks largely to the reopening of several large theaters in what city officials have dubbed the "North Loop Theater District." The **Chicago Theater** (at 175 North State Street), one of the grandest showplaces and once the heart of downtown social life, was renovated and reopened in 1986. The newly refurbished **Ford Center for the Performing Arts/Oriental Theater** (24 West Randolph Street) is attracting major Broadway musicals, as is the **Shubert Theater** (22 West Monroe Street). Up-and-coming are multimillion-dollar renovations to the Palace Theater in the Hotel Allegro (171 West Randolph Street) and the opening of the Goodman Theatre's new home on Dearborn and Randolph streets in fall 2000.

If you're walking through the Loop longing for someplace lush and quiet to sit for a moment and get your bearings, slip into the **Amoco Building** (200 East Randolph Street) and enjoy the quiet indoor garden atrium. While you're there, you might want to take a look at the *Sound Sculpture* on the east side of the building. This work of art, along with many more large public pieces displayed throughout the Loop, embody the city's commitment to beautifying the downtown area with sculpture, mosaics, and other open-air artwork.

Most notable among the downtown Loop sculptures are the Picasso sculpture (unnamed) in the plaza of **Richard J. Daley Center** (Dearborn Street between Randolph and Washington); Miró's *Chicago*, across the street from the Daley Center; and Marc Chagall's *Four Seasons* mosaic in **First Chicago Plaza** (near the corner of Dearborn and Monroe streets). Alexander

---

A Flamingo, a Pig, and Picasso's Wife

In 1967, when the city acquired the now-famous Picasso sculpture that stands outside Daley Center, it made a commitment to acquire great, large works of art to beautify the streetscapes. Three decades later, there are hundreds of sculptures and works of art on public display in Chicago. In the Loop, don't miss the unnamed Picasso (said to be modeled after a combination of a pig and one of his wives, poor thing!), Miró's *Chicago*, Alexander Calder's *Flamingo*, and Chagall's *Four Seasons*.

Calder's bright red *Flamingo* swings in the stark Federal Center plaza on Dearborn Street (between Jackson and Adams). For a few dollars you can pick up the *Loop Sculpture Guide* at the Chicago Cultural Center and spend hours combing the streets for the city's many monuments to creative achievement.

The Financial District

Much of the city's financial action takes place on the LaSalle Street corridor (or "canyon," as it's called), the Midwest's answer to Wall Street. The **Chicago Board of Trade** — located at the foot of LaSalle Street at 141 West Jackson — is one of two

Calder's "Flamingo" (1974), one of Chicago's many public artworks.

Chicago locations where live trading, done by an elaborate hand-signaling system, can be seen from an observation deck far above the crowd. This is the world's oldest futures exchange, where financiers have been gesticulating in a wild dance for money since 1848. If you want to understand what's going on, workers on the observation deck overlooking the trading pit offer brief explanations on the hour, and there's also a 16-minute audio-visual presentation. On your way out, take note of the building's Art Deco styling; a 31-ft (9½ m) statue of the goddess Ceres, the Roman goddess of grain and harvest, sits on top of the 45-story structure.

By the end of the day, the Chicago Mercantile Exchange can look like a trade wind blew across the trading floor.

The **Chicago Mercantile Exchange** (30 South Wacker Drive) offers curious visitors another live-action trading show. Traders here also wear bright jackets and looks of grim determination on their faces as they trade pork bellies, cattle, grain, and other perishables. This building also has an observation deck for visitors and offers a good view of the Chicago River as well.

While the financial district may offer a few dizzying moments for visitors, there's no doubt that the building most likely to make your knees go weak is the **Sears Tower** (occupying the block bounded by Wacker Drive and Franklin, Adams, and Jackson streets). At 110 stories, the Sears Tower is the tallest office building in the world, and on a clear day its Skydeck offers a panoramic view of the city, four states, and of course Lake Michigan. It takes Skydeck express elevators only 70 seconds to go from the ground floor to the observation destination 1,353 ft (412 m) above ground. Here's a tip: do what many kids long to and bypass the introductory 15-minute film at lobby level—just jump right on the elevator. Because the building was designed to sway up to three feet (about one meter) in the wind, visitors claim to have felt the movement on particularly blustery days. But on most days the Skydeck is simply one of the most incredible places to stand in the city.

Grant Park and the Museum Campus

If you have only one day in Chicago and shopping isn't your main objective, go to Grant Park's 300 acres (121 hectares) of open green space along Lake Michigan, take in the panoramic views of the city skyline, and spend a few hours in the three cultural jewels that comprise the centerpiece of the new Museum Campus. The Field Museum, Shedd Aquarium, and Adler Planetarium truly have some of the most fascinating exhibits in the entire country, suitably hands-on for kindergartners, detailed enough for adults.

Grant Park

Grant Park, which runs along Lake Michigan from (rough-ly) Randolph Street to Roosevelt Road, was conceived by

---

Downtown Parking

There are three underground parking facilities at Grant Park. They are a good bargain for the downtown area and fairly safe. There are several entrances along Michigan Avenue, Jackson Boulevard, and East Monroe Drive. At Monroe Street Underground Parking, you can park all day for one flat fee. If you've rented a car, park here for Loop excursions and for outings in Grant Park.

37

millionaire Montgomery Ward, took twenty years to complete, and opened in conjunction with the 1933–1934 "Century of Progress" Exposition. Today there are bike and pedestrian paths, one public and two private marinas dotting the waterfront with boats in summer, softball and baseball fields, flower gardens, a playground, a roller rink, and a general aura of urban beauty.

Petrillo Music Shell, near the north end of the park, is center stage for the city's many popular outdoor festivals in the summer. It is also home to the Grant Park Symphony Orchestra's summer season from mid-June through mid-August. The **Taste of Chicago** brings hundreds of Chicago restaurants to the park, with surprisingly haute cuisine represented. Millions of people come out for these city-sponsored events; they are free, relatively safe fun for the whole family.

Buckingham Fountain is a Grant Park highlight. Modeled after Bassin de Latone at Versailles and given to the city in 1927, the fountain is sculpted with four groups of whimsical sea horses and shoots dozens of water jets more than 100 ft (30 m) in the air. On evenings from May through October (until 11pm nightly), it is illuminated by more than 800 multicolored lights in a lovely timed light show. Street entertainers often contribute to the festival-like atmosphere at the base of the fountain, and a recent remodeling added a new café and pizzeria with outdoor seating

Earth, Sea, and Sky: The Museum Campus

The city is tremendously proud of what it is calling the new **Museum Campus**, and with good reason. For years, Lake Shore Drive divided the Field Museum from the Shedd Aquarium and Adler Planetarium, forcing visitors to walk from one cultural attraction to its neighbors through a dank underground pedestrian tunnel. Rerouting of Lake Shore

Onlookers gather at Buckingham Fountain on summer nights to watch colored lights play on the dancing water.

Drive and complete re-landscaping of the 57 acres (23 hectares) that join the Museum Campus's three cultural attractions cost $110 million and took ten years to complete. Now it's a unique urban space with sweeping lawns, tiered gardens, and free outdoor summer programs. It also makes a lot of sense: the scientific institutions are finally linked as one destination, as they should be.

You can reach the museum campus by taxi from the Loop for about $6, or by car. Ample parking is available as long as there's no major event at neighboring Soldier Field stadium. You also can take CTA bus #12 from the Roosevelt Road "El" station, and the campus is planning to run a free trolley shuttle from the "El" during summer months. If you come on rollerblades, you can check your wheels at a free valet area on the northeast corner outside the Field Museum; there are also ample bike racks.

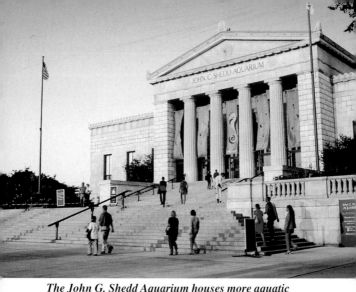

The John G. Shedd Aquarium houses more aquatic animals than any other location worldwide.

The **Field Museum** is a spectacle of grandeur for approaching motorists. A magnificent white marble, colonnaded building that faces north on Lake Shore Drive, it was built in the early 1920s with money from department store magnate Marshall Field. You can't miss this building, and you shouldn't miss what's inside either. One of the world's greatest institutions for the study of the earth and its peoples, the Field Museum has the largest Egyptian mummy collection outside of Cairo—an exhibit complete with a walk-through replica of an Egyptian tomb near the museum's south entrance. The North American Indian room has a life-sized Pawnee earth lodge, and Dinosaur Hall on the upper level now has a fossil laboratory exhibiting work in progress. The museum also has world-renowned exhibits on cultures of the Pacific, East Asia, Mexico, Central America, and Africa; on mammals of Asia; and on precious stones in the splendid Hall of Gems.

The **John G. Shedd Aquarium**, built in 1929 on the edge of Lake Michigan, recently added a spectacular $42-million Oceanarium that overlooks the water and creates the illusion of watching the daily dolphin shows somewhere along the northern coast of the Pacific Ocean. The aquarium is a mesmerizing introduction to aquatic animals, boasting the world's largest collection of marine life. There are sharks, several white whales, sea otters, and exotic eels, plus a nature trail, a naturalistic replica of the Falkland Island environment, and countless exhibits housing more than 8,000 aquatic animals. The Caribbean Reef exhibit, closed for a six-month renovation, reopened in Spring 1999 to feature a spectacular re-creation of a coral reef in a 90,000-gallon habitat. The aquarium also has a food court and restaurant.

Exit the aquarium and walk toward Lake Michigan along the Solidarity Drive peninsula, to the **Adler Planetarium and Astronomy Museum**. The planetarium's new Sky Pavilion is a multimillion-dollar project which the planetarium hopes will take its facility to new levels of popularity. The new wing includes a digital sky show and an interactive virtual-reality environment using revolutionary projection technology to take audiences to the edge of the universe. The Sky Pavilion's four new galleries feature the Milky Way, the solar system, and a "Big Bang" show that is part of the Chicago Millennium Celebration.

The Museum Campus is undeniably grand and can be a bit overwhelming. Don't try to do everything in a day: you'll need at least a few hours for each museum, and you should leave yourself time to linger in a quiet spot with a view of the lake. While you're there you might watch the small aircraft coming

Chicago Museum Highlights

Many museums in Chicago offer free admission one day each week, and several also are open on select evenings. Most are closed at least one day a week (often Monday) and on major holidays. Call ahead for holiday schedules, special events, and exhibits. Informative links to the city's many museums can be found at the official visitors' website at www.ci.chi.il.us/tourism.

Adler Planetarium and Astronomy Museum *1300 South Lake Shore Drive, on the Museum Campus; Tel. (312) 922-7827.* The first planetarium of its kind in the western hemisphere, the Adler features state-of-the-art sky shows and interactive exhibits on the solar system, galaxies, and stars. Open Monday–Thursday 9am–5pm, Friday until 9pm, Saturday and Sunday 9am–6pm. Admission: adults $5, children $4; free on Tuesdays.

Art Institute of Chicago *111 South Michigan Avenue; Tel. (312) 443-3600.* One of the great art museums, renowned for its outstanding collections that include some of the most famous paintings in the world. Exhibits cover Asian, African, and Oceanic art as well as Western art from ancient to contemporary. Open Monday–Friday 10:30am–4:30pm, Tuesday until 8pm, Saturday 10am–5pm, Sunday noon–5 pm. Suggested admission: adults $8, students/children/seniors $5; free on Tuesdays.

Chicago Children's Museum *700 East Grand Avenue (on Navy Pier); Tel. (312) 527-1000.* A lively, noisy, hands-on exploratorium, best suited for children aged 10 and under. Open Tuesday–Sunday 10am–5pm, Wednesday until 8pm. Admission: $6.50 per person; free on Thursdays 5pm–8pm.

DuSable Museum of African American History *740 East 56th Place; Tel. (773) 947-0600.* A South Side community institution dedicated to preserving and interpreting the experiences and achievements of African Americans, with regular exhibits of art, textiles, and history. Open Monday–Saturday 10am–5pm, Sunday noon–5pm. Admission: adults $3, seniors/students $2, children $1.

Field Museum *on Museum Campus, South Lake Shore Drive; Tel. (312) 922-9410.* One of the leading natural history museums in the world, filled with lively, educational, and ever-evolving interactive exhibits of more than 20 million cultural objects. Open daily, 9am–5pm. Admission: adults $7, seniors/children/students $4; free on Wednesdays.

Mexican Fine Arts Center Museum *1852 West 19th Street; Tel. (312) 738-1503.* The largest facility of its kind in the US, this museum offers a broad range of exhibits on Mexican visual and performing arts, from both within and outside Mexico. Open Tuesday–Sunday 10am–5pm. Free admission.

Museum of Contemporary Art *220 East Chicago Avenue; Tel. (312) 280-2660.* Chicago's newest major museum is just a few steps from the Water Tower and the Magnificent Mile. housing a provocative collection of contemporary painting, sculpture, photography, video, and film. Open Tuesday–Sunday 10am–5pm, Wednesday until 8pm. Admission: adults $6.50, seniors/students $4; free on first Tuesday of the month.

Museum of Science and Industry *57th Street and South Lake Shore Drive; Tel. (773) 684-1414, 800-GO-TO-MSI (toll-free).* A vast museum of international renown. Travel down into a coal mine, enter and tour a captured German U-505 World War II submarine, see the Apollo 8 spacecraft, and walk through a model of the human heart. Open Monday–Friday 9:30am–4pm, Saturday and Sunday 9:30am–5:30pm. Admission: adults $7, seniors $6, children $3.50; free on Thursdays.

Nature Museum *corner of Fullerton Parkway and Cannon Drive, in Lincoln Park; Tel. (773) 549-0606.* The stunning new home of the Chicago Academy of Sciences is an indoor-outdoor museum, with such state-of-the-art exhibits as a live butterfly haven, a wilderness walk, and a children's gallery. Open daily 10am–5pm (until 6pm in summer), Wednesdays until 8pm. Admission: adults $5, seniors/students $3; free on Tuesdays.

Shedd Aquarium *1200 South Lake Shore Drive, on the Museum Campus; Tel. (312) 939-2438.* See aquatic life from around the world in a variety of natural habitat exhibits, including three beluga whales, dolphins, harbor seals, and more than 8,000 other fascinating species. Open daily 9am–5pm (until 6pm June–August). Admission: adults $11 adults, children/seniors $9; free on Mondays (except for the Oceanarium, which has reduced admission on Mondays).

and going at **Meigs Field**, built on a peninsula in the lake below the planetarium. Just to the south of the Museum Campus are **Soldier Field** stadium and **McCormick Place Conference Center**, the world's largest exhibition and convention facility.

The Prairie District Museums

Also in the area are several smaller-scale museums, more limited in scope but offering unique appeal to visitors interested in their specialties. Take a footbridge west across Lake Shore Drive at the southern corner of the Museum Campus and find yourself in the **Prairie Avenue Historic District**, where the city's elite once lived. A cluster of architecturally beautiful 19th-century mansions are preserved here and open for tours. The most popular and impressive are the **Glessner Historic House Museum** (1800 South Prairie) and the **Clark Historic House Museum** (1855 South Indiana), landmark institutions that present slices of history and display authentic period architecture and interiors.

You might also want to visit the **National Vietnam Veterans Art Museum**, at 1801 South Indiana Avenue, which houses a growing collection of art created by veterans from around the world as well as artifacts from the war: three floors of haunting, angry, moving works of art that illuminate the human impact of the war in Vietnam. The **American Police Center and Museum** is also nearby, at 1717 South State Street.

Printers' Row

A small but distinct neighborhood just south of the Loop and west of Grant Park, **Printers' Row** is a corridor just north of the old Dearborn Street Station that was once the heart of printing and publishing in Chicago. Today it is best known as the setting for the annual **Printers' Row Bookfair**, a week-long outdoor event generally in late May/early June that attracts book lovers and sellers from throughout the Chicagoland area and beyond. There are a few lovely hotels in this area, and it's a great place to stay: convenient to the Loop, museums, and "El" stops, chic enough to be surrounded by new loft-condo apartments, but far enough from the Magnificent Mile so that you're not paying downtown prices for hotels or tourist rates at the restaurants.

North Michigan Avenue and the Gold Coast

Many visitors to Chicago begin their explorations on North Michigan Avenue, on the promenade known as the "**Magnificent Mile**." This is the city's most fashionable district, where the shopping invites favorable comparisons with New York's Fifth Avenue, minus (most of) the panhandlers.

There's something for everyone in the many shops and malls of the "Magnificent Mile."

Here you'll find the heart of the Heartland's most upscale shopping center, where you can shop at Henri Bendel, Gucci, Mondi, Saks Fifth Avenue, Bloomingdale's, Marshall Field's, Bigsby & Kruthers, Burberry, Niketown, and many, many more big-name merchandisers. The blocks are filled with the luxurious vertical malls, and the streetscapes are lined with upscale merchandising windows. East off Michigan, toward the lake's outer harbor, are some of the city's most expensive high-rise and condominium apartments, a neighborhood that emerged from what was once a hodgepodge of breweries, shipyards, factories, and immigrant slums. West of Michigan Avenue is an area of boutiques, nightclubs, restaurants, and theaters.

Oak Street and Rush Street

The top of the Magnificent Mile begins at **Oak Street**, where the Drake hotel—a crown jewel of the city that has hosted Prince Charles of England and other dignitaries—overlooks Lake Shore Drive. Tourists and locals alike crowd the streets of **North Michigan Avenue** dressed in their elegant best, or moving fast in running shoes and stereo headphones. The pace can be hectic and crossing the streets can mean jogging in a steady stream of buses, cabs, and noisy cars. On Saturday mornings or weekdays during rush hour, you'll be jostling elbows with tourists, shoppers, and commuters.

For a quick escape and a few minutes' peace, duck into the underground passageway to the Oak Street Beach and lakefront promenade, or stop for a moment of contemplation in the peaceful gardens of the **Fourth Presbyterian Church** between Chestnut Street and Delaware Place.

Walking west (away from the lake) on Oak Street brings you to fashionable boutiques and then to **Rush Street**. Once the haunt of college students and young professionals looking for a wild time in a few solid blocks of singles bars and loud eateries,

Rush Street is now a destination for out-of-town business people, tourists, and the very youngest set seeking a place to "party hearty." Women can often drink free here, and on weekends music pours into the streets like stale beer.

A few steps west of the lively Rush Street scene is the austere **Newberry Library**, on Walton Street between Dearborn Parkway and Clark Street. This quiet oasis is a paradise for bibliophiles and scholars: 1.6 million volumes in a rich collection spanning philosophy, art, religion, and other fields from the time that words were first printed. It is a research facility, not a circulating library.

The Gold Coast

With its proximity to the lakefront, green parklands, and downtown business areas, Astor Street and the surrounding tony boulevards of the **Gold Coast** (hugging the lakefront from around Oak Street up to North Avenue) were home to Chicago's high society in the late 1800s. Today the grand mansions on these streets are historic landmarks, standing as perpetual monuments to their owners' affluence.

This is a lovely place to see the beautiful Burberry set walking their impeccably groomed dogs. Elegant residential buildings with doormen are everywhere in the Gold Coast, and you can't really go wrong in any of the bistros or cafés in this neighborhood. Stroll along these blocks and step into a refined world where the homes are architecturally stunning and beautifully landscaped. Don't miss the 11-room **Charnley House** at 1365 Astor, designed by Frank Lloyd Wright early in his career.

The Hancock Building and the Water Tower

If you pause to look skyward anywhere in the neighborhood, you're sure to see the **John Hancock Center and Observatory** (875 North Michigan Avenue). With its observation deck

The view from the Hancock building's observation deck: if it weren't for the fog, you'd see clear to Wisconsin.

on the 94th floor, the Hancock building is the third-tallest structure in Chicago. While many folks want to see the world from atop the slightly taller Sears Tower in the city's financial district, the Hancock's open-air deck offers wonderful views of Lake Michigan and the surrounding metropolis. On a clear day you can see all the way to the shores of neighboring states Indiana, Michigan, and Wisconsin. The Observatory is open every day until midnight and features 3-D "talking" tele-

scopes that speak in four languages and an outside skywalk (safely screened).

The modern Hancock building stands in stark contrast to the quaint Gothic **Water Tower** just a few blocks south. With your head out of the clouds and your feet on the ground, walk back almost 100 years to the Water Tower Visitor's Center on the corner of Michigan and Chicago avenues, across Michigan from the original Water Tower structure itself. Built of local yellow limestone in 1869, the Water Tower is one of the few buildings to have survived the Chicago Fire of 1871, and it remains perhaps the city's most enduring symbol. Inside the Visitor's Center are a café and an office that sells tickets (often at half-price) to the city's theatrical and musical events (see page 126).

If you need a meeting point, or a park bench to sit on while you look at your map, the small grassy park area around Water Tower is just the place—as long as you don't mind sharing it with pigeons, noisy youngsters, and other out-of-towners doing exactly the same. If you're looking for a horse-drawn carriage ride, this is the area where many liveries wait.

Across the street from the real Water Tower is the one that's most on Chicagoans' lips these days: **Water Tower**

Place, the flagship vertical shopping mall here on North Michigan Avenue. A branch of the Marshall Field's department store anchors the stunning complex, which you enter via a dramatic atrium with fountains and a sweeping escalator ride up into the mall's first level.

Art and Commerce on North Michigan

The bustling city blocks between Oak Street and the Chicago River to the south also house several top-notch hotels, some small eateries, and a few high-priced art galleries. But for a true artistic experience in this part of town, visit the Terra Museum or the Museum of Contemporary Art.

The **Terra Museum of American Art** (664 North Michigan Avenue) is a recent cultural addition to the commercial hubbub of the Magnificent Mile. It can be a welcome respite from the onslaught of see-and-spend mentality that holds many Michigan Avenue wanderers in its sway. The Terra is designed much like the Whitney in New York, with plenty of open space surrounding a central spiral staircase, an impressive permanent collection of works from 1800 to the present, and special exhibits featuring work of American artists at home and abroad.

The **Museum of Contemporary Art** (220 East Chicago Avenue) is housed in an impressive new $46-million building a few steps off Michigan Avenue next to the Water Tower Place shopping center. The collection is ever-growing, and the museum has hands-on workshop projects for children and families every weekend, plus performance art in its 300-seat theater and a lovely sculpture garden.

As you get closer to the Chicago River, North Michigan Avenue has upper and lower decks, which keep commercial traffic and truck deliveries out of sight. One of the few reasons to venture below is to pop into the **Billy Goat Tavern**, made famous by a "Saturday Night Live" TV skit featuring John Belushi in the role of the counter chef, crying "Chee-burger, chee-burger!" and "No fries—chips!" The scruffy tavern is actually across the street from the *Chicago Tribune* building and only a few blocks from the *Chicago Sun-Times* offices, reportedly a popular spot for hard-core reporters looking for a cheap meal and a little gossip.

The tabloid paper for the city that works, it's not surprising that the *Chicago Sun-Times* has its massive printing presses on view for visitors. If flying ink and breaking news are your idea of a good time, walk over to the **Chicago Sun-Times Building** on North Wabash at the river and take a look at the ancient machinery pounding out the day's headlines.

For a more civilized view of the news, you can stand outside **Tribune Tower** (at 435 North Michigan Avenue, just north of the river) and look in at WGN Radio's street-level studios or watch a steady stream of news scroll ticker-tape style across an electronic screen. The Tribune Tower was built after its Gothic design was selected from more than 600 entries submitted for a architectural contest in 1922. At the base of the tower, take a minute to find the stones built into the structure from other famous buildings and monuments. Legend has it that *Chicago Tribune* owner Col. Robert McCormick had his reporters send or lug them back from famous structures around the world.

> On Wacker Drive you can go east or west along the Chicago River, north or south along the river branch, and ride on the upper or lower deck. If you're going someplace on Wacker, be sure to figure out the cross-street. If you're in a car, you can avoid a lot of traffic by traveling on Lower Wacker Drive.

The Tribune Tower and the much-photographed **Wrigley Building** across the street mark what is roughly the end of the Magnificent Mile. As you step onto the **Michigan Avenue Bridge**, pause to look north across the skyline, or west over the river. From here you can see the twin cylindrical buildings that make up **Marina City Towers**. These structures, built in 1964, boast condos, parking garages, grocery stores, a bowling alley, a bank, and more, so that residents need never leave if they don't want to. At the base of the buildings is the new House of Blues club and hotel. If loud and dark and "New Orleans influence" are your idea of a good time, put this destination on your after-dark agenda.

From the bridge you can also walk down a staircase on the northeastern corner and find yourself on the river esplanade. Below the noise and rush at street level, the riverwalk that leads toward Lake Michigan can be a lovely place in warmer months.

> **The city's public radio station is WBEZ, 91.5 FM, which broadcasts live from Navy Pier.**

If you're enjoying the views, walk a few blocks east to the edge of **Centennial Fountain** (on the river esplanade, east of McClurg Court), built to commemorate the reversal of the Chicago River's flow in 1900.

If you're standing over the river in March, look down at the water: the city colors it green for St. Patrick's Day.

☞ Navy Pier

Since it opened as a shipping and recreational facility in 1916, **Navy Pier** has been a Chicago landmark. A major overhaul to the pier in the early 1990s created an indoor-outdoor recreational facility and mall similar to Baltimore's Inner Harbor and New York's South Street Seaport. This is a place where you can spend a whole day, especially if you like your entertainment prepackaged. There are dozens of eateries, scores of small shops, a museum, the Navy Pier IMAX movie theater, an indoor pavilion with live entertainment, sightseeing boats on the wharf at the ready, and lots more. It takes only a few steps to go from a specialty store to a seafood-and-gumbo

Navy Pier lights up the Chicago night with rides, games, food, shows, and other attractions.

eatery and then on to the outdoor Ferris wheel. This is the kind of place some people find stimulating, while others think it too commercial to be truly enjoyable.

The pier is on Lake Michigan at the east end of Grand Avenue, between Ohio and Illinois streets. Access to the pier is free, although getting there is a bit of a trip. Don't try to walk from the Loop or from the downtown shopping area unless you're feeling very energetic. There's plenty of public transportation that will get you there easily (see page 55).

A state-of-the-art fountain marks the entrance to Navy Pier. **Dock Street**, which runs the length of the pier's South Dock, is reserved for pedestrians as well as bicyclists and joggers. In summer months jugglers, mimes, stilt-walkers, comedians, singers, and musicians give the pier an exciting

The quintessential Chicago experience: admiring the view from the Sears Tower, the tallest building in the US.

festival ambiance. Dinner-cruise ships operate from Dock Street, and the pier puts on a nice fireworks display on select holiday evenings in the summer.

If you make it to the pier, absolutely do pay the small fee and ride the **Ferris wheel**. This ride is 150 ft (46 m) high and modeled after the world's very first Ferris wheel, which was built for Chicago's 1893 World Columbian Exposition. The wheel turns continuously, slowly enough for riders to step into one of the 40 oversized gondolas as it is moving. An unobtrusive narrative describing the skyline is piped into each gondola, and in the evening the ride is lit by thousands of lights. In fall and winter there is an open-air ice rink under the Ferris wheel. Skate a bit and then relax in the **Crystal Gardens** at the far end of the indoor pavilion. This botanical oasis under an enormous glass atrium is full of dancing fountains, palm trees, and public seating.

The **Chicago Children's Museum** is a major attraction, occupying three levels and attracting hundreds of thousands of families to its interactive exhibits for young people every year. Among the most innovative are the "Water Ways" display, which lets children experiment with rerouting and pumping water into a large aquatic system, and the "Climbing Schooner,"

Where Else but Chicago?

In addition to its world-class museums, theaters, and cultural institutions, Chicago boasts unique attractions that will have something to please everyone. Here are three of the most popular:

Navy Pier takes you right onto the lake at the foot of Grand Avenue, with more than 50 acres of parks, promenades, gardens, shops, restaurants, and special rides and attractions. Navy Pier is open 365 days a year, 10am to 10pm. There is free trolley service along Grand Avenue from the subway station at State Street: look for the blue Navy Pier Trolley signs. Or you can ride one of the following CTA bus routes: #29, #56, #65, #66, #120, or #121. Call for more information: Tel. (312) 595-PIER.

Lincoln Park Zoo is imaginatively designed, easy to navigate, manageable in a day, and always free to the public: it's one of the best bargains in the city. Open 365 days a year, 9am to 5 pm; admission is free. Parking is available for $7. Accessible via the #151 or #156 bus routes. For information: Tel. (312) 742-2000.

Sears Tower Skydeck is the public observatory atop the tallest building in the US. It can be reached from the street-level entrance on Jackson Boulevard between Franklin Street and Wacker Drive. The Skydeck is open seven days a week, 9am to 10pm (until 11pm March through September). Admission is $8.50 for adults, $5.50 for children; a family pass is $21. For information: Tel. (312) 875-9696.

connecting floor levels with an maze that tests dexterity and bravery as kids enter on one level and emerge on the next.

On weekend afternoons the restaurants on the pier are crowded, but there's always room at the absolutely enormous McDonald's. If you can get in, enjoy the live jazz and spicy southern food at Joe's Be-Bop Café and Jazz Emporium, and if you're up for fine dining you should make a reservation and go to Riva, where you can enjoy waterfront views.

River North

Cross the Chicago River from the Loop, or walk west from the Magnificent Mile, and you'll find yourself in one of the city's most active night spots. After dark, Lincoln Park, Wicker Park, and other North Side neighborhoods are generally for people in their 20s and 30s, but **River North** is for all.

Art galleries, theme restaurants, suburbanites, and out-of-towners are what River North is all about. In the area roughly defined by the Chicago River on the west and south, Clark Street on the east, and Oak Street on the north, the galleries rival Rock n' Roll McDonald's, Rainforest Café, and Hard Rock Café as a center of activity. With one restaurant after another, **Ontario Street** could be called "Calorie Row." Some eateries here are better than others: if there's a neon-light cluster outside, your best bet is probably something made from potatoes.

If you like a big, loft-life dining experience where the food is good and the people-watching is excellent, try Scoozi! (on the corner of Orleans and Hubbard streets). One of the many larger-than-life eateries in the popular "Lettuce Entertain You" group of restaurants (known for their distinct décor and the buzz they create), Scoozi! has been popular with Chicagoans since it opened in 1986.

A few steps from the eating crowd you'll find the **River North Gallery District**. The greatest concentration of art galleries in Chicago can be found here—more than 60 within a one-mile radius from the intersection of Superior and Franklin streets. Poseurs and art aficionados alike come out the first Friday of every month for the galleries' cocktail hours. Works by the Midwest's most promising artists can be admired or purchased in these storefront galleries.

The **Merchandise Mart** (the nation's second-largest building, after the Pentagon) stands on the river between Franklin and Wells streets. Its size alone is impressive. Predominantly a wholesale market serving the upscale home furnishings industry, there is a series of shops and eateries open to the public on the lower floors.

One of the greatest ironies of the city is right here, where some of Chicago's most elite addresses and top tourist destinations (in River North and the Gold Coast, and in Old Town to the north) are only a short distance from the city's infamous **Cabrini-Green** housing projects. Built in the late 1950s in a district north of Chicago Avenue and west of Orleans Street, Cabrini-Green is a 15-tower neighborhood that has spawned and nurtured some of the city's worst drug problems and gang rivalries. The city has slowly been demolishing these towers, and developers are building expansive residences in their place, but the process won't be complete until well into the new century. Today it's even a bad idea to drive by in your car; the area should be avoided when visiting the neighboring River North and Old Town districts.

> Unlike drivers in many pedestrian-hostile cities, cars generally will yield in Chicago if you cross in the middle of the road. Buses and taxis are, of course, another story…

THE NORTH SIDE

North of downtown, the city's neighborhoods and shopping districts spread like a checkerboard, reflecting the patterns of immigration and economic development of the past hundred years. On the **North Side** you'll find some of the trendiest restaurants and theater companies located on blocks that are rather drab and nondescript in the daytime but become lively entertainment centers at night. Here, too, you can find historic little Wrigley Field —major league baseball's leafy gem—as well as the pleasures and recreation offered by Lincoln Park and the beaches and harbors that stretch north to the city's suburban borders.

Lincoln Park and Old Town

One of the most popular neighborhoods in the city, **Lincoln Park** can be an antidote to too much time spent in downtown museums and mega-stores. Not that it's quiet here. This part of the city is up partying until the wee hours of the morning in the blues and jazz clubs that line Lincoln Avenue—and

See an ark's worth of animals for free at the lovely Lincoln Park Zoo.

then out jogging at dawn. If you love the soulful sound of a trumpet (and don't mind a crowd), you won't want to miss the scene at Kingston Mines or B.L.U.E.S. But you might also enjoy watching the sun come up over the lake on a peaceful Sunday morning. You can do it all in the Lincoln Park neighborhood, in relative safety. This is a 'round-the-clock area with a manageable pace and friendly ambiance.

The neighborhood that Chicagoans call "Lincoln Park" runs along Lake Michigan roughly from Armitage Avenue to Diversey Parkway, and as far west as Clybourn Avenue. Two of the city's diagonal, grid-defying roads (Clark Street and Lincoln Avenue) are the major thoroughfares on which much of the action takes place. Fullerton and Webster streets are also busy night and day. But the heart and origin of this area will always be the park that gives the neighborhood its name.

The Park

Lincoln Park itself actually begins at about North Avenue and ends up at Diversey Avenue, but parklands and beaches continue along the lake nearly to the city's northern border. With grassland, beaches, soccer fields, harbors, the lakefront promenade, golf course, and tennis courts, Lincoln Park is a great place to take a stroll, sunbathe, or people-watch.

Begin your visit at the **Lincoln Park Zoo**. The zoo is an incredibly popular destination, and for good reason: it's free, it's lovely, and it's very accessible. You can see the entire 35 acres (14 hectares) in a few hours—from the fabulous Bird House to the Great Ape House, and from the dell and gladed Rookery to the African and Asian giants in the Large Mammal Area. Feeding time is fun in the Penguin/Seabird House, and some children take special delight in watching the vampire bats get their daily dish of blood in the Small Mammal/Reptile House. The Farm in the Zoo is a wonderful place for kids to have an up-close-and-personal experience with barnyard animals, and the Kovler Lion House is filled with majestic felines. In season, paddleboats can be rented at the lake outside Café Brauer.

At the north end of the zoo, on Fullerton Avenue and Stockton Drive, **Lincoln Park Conservatory** is absolutely splendid in any season, but the acres of exotic plant life in this landmark glass atrium are especially beautiful in February, April, mid-November, and late December, when they are filled with flowers. Like the zoo, the conservatory is open daily, and is always free.

Diagonally across Fullerton Avenue behind the conservatory, you'll find the state-of-the-art **Nature Museum** of the Chicago Academy of Sciences. The new $31-million home for this veteran institution relocates the 141-year-old organization to a sweeping new facility overlooking the lake, with indoor-outdoor exhibits designed to connect people with nature and the environment.

The **Chicago Historical Society**, at the far south end of Lincoln Park near the corner of Clark Street and North Avenue (where Old Town meets the Gold Coast), is a lively, interactive memorial to the city's history and the nation's evolution. Its exhibits range from high culture to low-brow politics, railroads to meat packing. Special events are enjoyed by Chicagoans throughout the year, and visitors are welcome to join the walking tours and other events. If you're curious about the Great Chicago Fire or any other aspect of historical significance to the city, this is the place to have your questions answered.

While you're in the area, swing onto Lincoln Avenue and walk north to see what's playing at the **Biograph Theater** (2433 North Lincoln Avenue). This is the spot where gangster John Dillinger was gunned down by the FBI in 1934, earning

The Lincoln Park Conservatory adds acres of flora to the neighboring zoo's acres of fauna.

it a place on the National Register of Historic Places. It's surrounded now by wonderful bookshops where bibliophiles can spend hours browsing among the old and new.

Lill Street Gallery (1021 West Lill Street, between Lincoln Avenue and Halsted Street) is worth a visit if you're a ceramics buff. This is the Midwest's largest ceramics center, providing working space to more than 40 local artists.

Old Town

From the historical society, walk west on North Avenue to Wells Street and you'll be in **Old Town**. This is the home to **Second City** (1616 North Wells Street), the improvisational comedy club that groomed such legends as Joan Rivers, the late John Belushi, and Bill Murray. Old Town has been many things in its day—a working-class German enclave in the 1850s, the center of folk music and "hippie" activities in the 1960s—and also home to some of the most expensive residences in the city. Take a stroll around the block of **Crilly Court**, where architecturally beautiful Queen Anne-style buildings from the 19th century are built with stunning old-world porches that you can see from a private alley.

The **Old Town School of Folk Music** (909 West Armitage Avenue) is a school and performance space that has been a neighborhood fixture since it was founded in 1957. You might want to stop in and see what eclectic performances coincide with your trip. Charlie Trotter's, a city bastion of fine cuisine, is right across the street.

Getting Funky: Lakeview, Wrigleyville, and Southport

These residential neighborhoods north of West Diversey Parkway are fun for walking, wandering, and hanging out, whether you have a specific destination or simply feel the yen to be out where the people live.

Lakeview is sometimes called "Boys' Town," a flashback to twenty years ago, when the gay community gentrified the area. Coffee shops, bookstores, antiques shops, and boutiques followed. Eventually the gay community moved farther north and west, yielding to an urban professional crowd just slightly less upscale than the one you'll find in Lincoln Park. There is a lot of nightlife here on North Clark and Halsted streets, especially along the blocks surrounding Wrigley Field, a little neighborhood that has taken the name "Wrigleyville."

One of the best places in the US to see a baseball game, **Wrigley Field** is an ivy-covered brick ballpark set right in the middle of a residential neighborhood, on the corner where Addison Street meets Clark Street. The home of the **Chicago Cubs** was built in 1914, but there were no night games here until 1988, when stadium lights were finally installed. Today you can sit in the bleachers and see a game day or night, then pop into one of the many sports bars along Clark Street and chug down some cold brews while listening to loud rock music with hundreds of other sports fans. There is an "El" station at Addison Street, so getting here is a snap.

Don't pass up the chance to see some of the funky retro shops along Belmont Avenue and Halsted Street. Definitely not for the straight-laced, these stores carry everything from kitschy kitchen tools to kinky love toys. Flashy Trash (3524 North Halsted Street) is one of the best shops in the city for new and used retro clothes. In a city rich with independent bookstores, nearby Unabridged Books (3251 North Broadway) is an undisputed favorite.

People also enjoy touring Chicago's **Graceland Cemetery** on the corner of Clark Street and Irving Park Road. This is the final resting spot for some of Chicago's biggest names, including railroad magnate George Pullman, city planner Daniel Burnham, and architects Louis Sullivan and Mies van der Rohe.

Exploring Old Town can be exciting, but if it looks like you've wandered into a different, less desirable neighborhood, you probably have. This part of the city borders some of Chicago's rougher areas, which are immediately to the west and to the south.

In the **Southport** neighborhood (west of Lakeview along Southport Avenue) you can start your afternoon bowling a few games at charming Southport Lanes (3325 North Southport), a renovated 75-year-old bowling alley where the pins are still set by hand. Pick up some interesting jewelry or international handiwork at Fourth World Artisans (3440 North Southport) up the block, or have a drink and a snack at Café Zinc (3443 North Southport), where the remarkable, silvery zinc bar was brought over from France. Then, you can catch a movie at the **Music Box Theater**, a beautiful fine-art theater in a landmark

1929 building at 3733 North Southport; an organist provides live entertainment between shows, and the ceiling in the larger 750-seat main room is afloat with clouds across a blue sky—or stars in a night sky, depending on the lighting.

Young and on the Edge: Wicker Park and Bucktown

Once enclaves to working class German and eastern European immigrants, these low-rent neighborhoods were discovered by artists, musicians, and young urbanites in the early 1980s. The Smashing Pumpkins rock band emerged from the music scene here. If you think body piercing is cutting edge, stick to Lakeview or Lincoln Park after dark; if you think it's practically mandatory for high style, hit Bucktown after midnight. In these adjacent neighborhoods west of the Kennedy Expressway, grunge, huge black boots, and retro styles unimaginable to most people over the age of 40 (picture poodle skirts and nose rings) are alive and very happening, at all hours of the day and night.

The center of activity is the intersection where Damen, North, and Milwaukee avenues meet: on the grid system that's 1600 North and 2000 West, which you might want to know, since the best way to get here at night from downtown is by cab or car. Bucktown is, roughly, north of the intersection, and Wicker Park is below it; the neighborhoods really blend together here.

From this traffic-jammed corner, the clubs and restaurants radiate in all directions. And with so many artists in the area, galleries and studios are plentiful. In the **Flat Iron Building** at Milwaukee and Damen, some of the resident artists welcome visitors to their studios on the upper floors. The best times to see the flourishing art scene is at the gallery show openings in late August or during the **Around the Coyote Arts Festival** in early September, when hundreds of Bucktown and Wicker Park artists open their lofts to the public.

The Occult Bookstore (1561 North Milwaukee) is worth a visit, whether it's for a hoot or for spiritual enlightenment. You can walk by and look at the **Nelson Algren House** (1958 West Evergreen Avenue), where the author lived and worked, but you can't go inside. The same is true of these neighborhoods' old mansions along West Caton Street and West Pierce and North Hoyne avenues. Known as the "ethnic Gold Coast," these blocks are lined with stunning houses built by wealthy immigrants in the 19th century. You can see many architectural styles here, from Italianate to Swiss Chalet. This is the true original Wicker Park neighborhood, a name that was co-opted and stretched by developers when the area began to gentrify.

It's only a quick cab ride from Wicker Park to the **Old World Ukrainian Village** neighborhood, but the difference is night and day. Ukrainian is spoken on the streets in this small enclave

Look, mom, henna'ed hands — a henna tattoo artist works her (temporary) magic.

that remains predominantly true to its roots. Notable places to see here are the **Ukrainian National Museum** (721 North Oakley Blvd.), the modest **Ukrainian Institute of Modern Art** (2320 West Chicago Avenue), and the intricate mosaics in the **St. Nicholas Ukrainian Catholic Cathedral** (2238 West Rice Street). This Byzantine-style cathedral was built in 1915 and has been a centerpiece of the community ever since.

THE WEST SIDE

Cross the south branch of the Chicago River from the Loop and you're in the most ethnically mixed area in the city. After its "peak" right after the Civil War, the mansions in this small, exclusive residential district were replaced by warehouses and markets, and the **West Side** subsequently sheltered the city's working immigrant poor. Today it's a strange mix of eclectic new restaurants and old ethnic neighborhoods.

West Loop

In this city of neighborhoods, some have endured for centuries while others seem to fade and then spring back to life at the drop of a name or the opening of a restaurant. The name that brought this area in the shadow of the Sears Tower into its current period of rejuvenation is "Oprah Winfrey." The superstar host of the popular TV talk-show brought her impressive studios to a renovated US armory building on West Washington Boulevard in 1988, and it didn't take long for the glitterati to follow with swanky restaurants, leather coats, and cellular phones. The place is now known as "West Loop."

From what was once the city's flower and meat warehouse district, at 1050 West Washington Boulevard, **Harpo Studios** ("Oprah" spelled backwards) tapes a daily show which is broadcast around the world to more than 15 million viewers, and welcomes the public to be the audience. You need a reservation to get in, and it's a good idea to call at least a month ahead (see page 120).

The same might be said about some of the area's restaurants, especially Blackbird, Bluepoint Oyster Bar, Toque, and Marché. Don't be surprised if your waiters have henna tattoos and an attitude. Dress in your starkest black and give the attitude right back to them: it's what they're expecting (along with a tip to match that hefty bill you're bound to run up).

Oprah Winfrey revitalized the West Loop with the construction of Harpo Studios.

Basketball star Michael Jordan is another local luminary whose name, face, and likeness in a soaring bronze statue in front of the city's new **United Center** sports stadium (West Madison Street between Damen and Paulina) have pushed the West Loop district into the limelight. Jordan's enormous career put the Bulls on the international map, and the recently retired superstar is also a principal investor in the nearby, plush new restaurant One Sixtyblue.

If you're in the area, be sure to stop into the **Museum of Holography** at 1134 West Washington Boulevard. This small but impressive collection of three-dimensional laser images is well worth a visit.

Greektown

Not far from the West Loop is a neighborhood still as genuine and old-fashioned as the Harpo Studios area is trendy. Here they shout "O-o-pah!" rather than "Oprah!" When you hear this cry it means a plate of flaming cheese is on its way to a table near you.

Known primarily for its restaurants, **Greektown** is south of the United Center sports arena and adjacent to the **University of Illinois at Chicago**. The campus has brought a few urban pioneers to a string of new townhouses and renovated loft apartments, but it hasn't spoiled the family-owned eateries. Generally the prices are reasonable and the service is friendly — and the flaming-cheese specialty, called *saganaki,* is salty but reliably good. If you're going to catch a Bulls basketball game or a Blackhawks ice hockey game at the stadium, bring your boisterous group to South Halsted Street and choose from among a dozen charming Greek restaurants.

Students are a common sight here, and while it's not particularly a tourist destination, anyone interested in the history of social work in America will enjoy a stop at the **Jane Addams Hull House Museum** on the university campus. In 1856 Addams set up a day-care facility and social service agency here to serve the needs of the city's poor immigrant families. Visitors today can see a preserved dining hall and a slide show detailing Addams's advocacy for child-labor laws and public education, which garnered her the Nobel Peace Prize in 1931.

Little Italy

Like Greektown, **Little Italy** is primarily a destination for hungry groups looking for a good meal at bargain prices. It is reported that before she opened her own restaurant (and began her perpetual diet), Oprah loved coming to Little Italy for the tasty food and large servings. While there are a few notable places to go for a hefty portion of pasta on Taylor Street, the area's housing projects and the presence of buzzers on many of the restaurants' doors discourage most visitors from venturing here unless a friend at the university is the draw.

THE SOUTH SIDE

The city below the Loop is vast and includes some neighborhoods of distinction, despite its reputation as "the baddest part of town." If you venture to the South Side, go directly to your chosen destination. A taxi cab, the Metra line commuter train, or the CTA's express bus #6 are the best ways to get to Hyde Park, where you'll find the illustrious University of Chicago and the ever-popular Museum of Science and Industry. Taking the CTA "El" trains to the South Side is not generally advised.

Hyde Park

The city's intellectual capital, **Hyde Park** is worth a trip, if walking through a stunning Neo-Gothic ivy-covered campus, sitting in a coffee-house debating the relevance of post-structuralism, and browsing through some of the best bookstores in the world is your idea of a fun day.

> Don't walk to the West Loop area; take a taxi-cab instead. They are easy to come by here, and the neighborhood between downtown and this chic strip is still fairly unpredictable, especially at night.

Do this in the daylight, not at night; even the students stand on stage at grungy Jimmy's Woodlawn Tap (one of the few places to go for a cold beer at this end of town, at 1172 East 55th Street) and read poetry about how scary it is to live here. Then they take a cab home if it's even close to twilight.

The **University of Chicago** is what made this part of town what it is today. It's been here since 1890, when John D. Rockefeller put up millions of dollars to jump-start the private institution. Today its schools, colleges, libraries, museums, and institutes comprise the 190-acre (77-hectare) campus, concentrated in the blocks between East 55th Street and East 60th Street, from Cottage Grove east to Woodlawn. Internationally

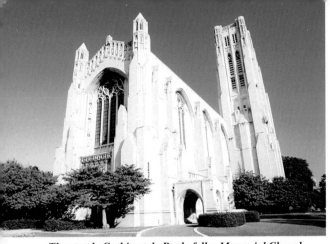

The stately Gothic-style Rockefeller Memorial Chapel houses the second-largest carillon in the world.

recognized as one of the foremost universities in the world, the "U of C" boasts a prestigious medical center and the site where Enrico Fermi and his team of scientists created the world's first self-sustaining controlled nuclear chain reaction in 1942.

Take a walking tour of the university area, beginning at **Robie House** (5757 South Woodlawn Avenue), a quintessential Prairie Style creation built in 1909 by Frank Lloyd Wright (see page 20) and now preserved as a museum. From here, walk over to the **Oriental Institute Museum** at 1155 East 58th Street, where you can see newly renovated galleries exhibiting art and artifacts from the Near East dating back to 9000 B.C. The stately Gothic architecture of the campus will undoubtedly draw you into the courtyard across South University Avenue, where you can see the Tower Group buildings, modeled after a college at Oxford University. The chimes that echo across campus come from these towers.

Rockefeller Memorial Chapel (5850 South Woodlawn Avenue, at 59th Street) houses the world's second-largest carillon, which you can hear all over the campus at frequent recitals; the building was completed in 1928.

From the courtyard, walk directly north, pass through the gargoyle-laden Cobb Gate, and you'll be right in front of the **Joseph Regenstein Library** (1100 East 57th Street), where the first floor is open to visitors during the day. Behind the library, at 5550 South Greenwood Avenue, is the **David and Alfred Smart Museum of Art**, which houses the university's art collection and has some impressive pieces by the likes of Degas, Matisse, Rodin, and many old masters.

Swing back down the block and across to East 58th Street, where you'll find what could well be the best bookstore in the world. **Seminary Co-op Bookstore** (5757 South University Avenue) is a catacomb-like warren of rooms serving the bracingly intellectual university community, stocking just about everything—except the mundane or the shoddily written bestseller. For more general interests, do not miss 57th Street Books (1301 East 57th Street), the co-op's mainstream sister store, or neighboring Powell's Bookstore (1501 East 57th Street).

If you get hungry around here, you might as well slip into the Medici for espresso or into Edwardo's for some pizza, as there are surprisingly few places to fill your belly in Hyde Park; everyone must be too busy stuffing themselves with knowledge instead.

To the west of the campus is enormous **Washington Park**. Follow the **Midway Plaisance** (a broad road with a wide centerpiece of grass, which runs south along the university), and you'll reach the **Fountain of Time** sculpture at the spot where the Midway meets the park. This dramatic concrete sculpture, erected in 1922, asks visitors to contemplate their own mortality and is one of the city's most moving public artworks.

The **DuSable Museum of African American History**, in the park at East 56th Place, is well worth a visit. Developed in 1961 to preserve and interpret the experiences and achievements of African Americans, the museum features a Hall of Fame honoring heroes from Frederick Douglass to Langston Hughes, an exhibit that traces the Civil Rights movement, and more than 90 works of art.

Science Museum and Surroundings

Tucked down along the lake at 57th Street and South Lake Shore Drive is one of the city's most popular cultural attractions, the **Museum of Science and Industry**. The building is what will strike you first. Built in 1893 as part of the World Columbian Exposition, it opened as a museum in 1933 and has been a major draw ever since.

With everything from high-tech lunar models and a recently updated ride that simulates an eerie descent into a coal mine to the chickens hatching in an incubator and a walk through a World War II-vintage submarine, this museum is absolutely exciting. "Science and industry" is an ambitiously broad undertaking for one institution, but this one does it with gusto. So much gusto, in fact, that the place can be a little overwhelming. Allow yourself plenty of time here, as you'll want to see as much of this 2,000-exhibit museum as possible.

Outside the museum are two points of interest. To the east, at Lake Michigan, is a rock jetty known as "the Point." Ambitious university faculty members swim in the small harbor these rocks create, and it is a great place for picnicking or just relaxing. To the south of the museum, across Columbia Drive, are the **Jackson Park lagoons** and its peaceful **Osaka Garden**, a meditative and tranquil spot with a new tea house, lanterns, and bridges. The park was designed by landscape architect Frederick Law Olmsted (designer also of New York

City's Central Park) to accommodate the same exposition that brought the museum's building and the Midway into existence.

Chinatown

South of the Loop, just a few blocks west of the McCormick Place Conference Center, is Chicago's modest **Chinatown**, complete with pagoda-style arches over the streets and large groups of local Asian customers in the area's restaurants. A large majority of the city's Asian population lives here, on real estate that has been rising in value and expanding the neighborhood's borders. Chinatown's center is, roughly, the triangle created by Wentworth, Cermak, and Archer avenues. You can get to Chinatown via the CTA "El" to Cermak Avenue.

There are no major attractions here, although the annual Chinese New Year Parade that runs along Wentworth and Cermak in February is a festive event in the neighborhood.

Designed by the man responsible for New York City's Central Park, the Osaka Garden is an oasis of tranquility.

Wandering through Chinatown is a fairly safe and certainly enjoyable experience. You can buy authentic Asian cooking tools, shop for food and produce in one of the many markets, or have a wonderful meal in a Chinese or Vietnamese restaurant. It's a good idea to brush up on your preferences—Cantonese style or Szechwan style—before you come. A word of caution: stick to the well-trafficked roads in Chinatown, and don't wander east of Wentworth Avenue, where a housing project makes the area between here and the Prairie Avenue Historic District less than safe for visitors.

Pilsen

The highlight of **Pilsen**, the vibrant immigrant neighborhood west of Chinatown, is undoubtedly the **Mexican Fine Arts Center Museum** (1852 West 19th Street), on the edge of Harrison Park. Opened in 1986, this innovative museum dedicated to the visual and performing arts of the Mexican and Latino cultures has a worldwide reputation for creative exhibits and programs. Painting, sculpture, textiles, and photography are part of the museum's growing permanent collection, enriched by a "sister museum" arrangement with El Museo del Templo Mayor in Mexico City. A new wing, completed in 1998, expanded the building to three times its original size.

If the museum draws you to this neighborhood off the river, you might also want to grab a bite to eat at one of the many taquerias, bakeries, or sidewalk food vendors. Pilsen is home base for the city's growing Mexican-American population but also has vestiges from the past, when Czech immigrants gave the area its name (for a town in the Czech Republic) and Polish, Serbian, and Croatian immigrants were attracted to the affordable housing and easy access to the "El." If you take the CTA Blue Line train here during the day, you'll know you're in the right place when you get off and see the 18th Street station, itself a work of art filled with Mexican- and Latino-inspired murals.

Pullman

On the far south end of Chicago is the **Pullman Historic District**. This area was nothing less than a small fiefdom built in 1880 by George Pullman, the man who invented the Pullman railway car. The town of Pullman was a community for Pullman Palace Car Company employees, where size and style of housing were accorded by rank. Pullman was heralded by the business and social leaders of his day until the violent strike of 1894, when the company reduced wages without reducing rents in the company town. This strike crippled the nation's railways and was a turning point in the history of the US labor movement. It embittered Pullman, who died just before his company was ordered by the courts to sell off the private community. The town of Pullman later became part of Chicago, although it is so far south (111th Street) it might as well be in another state.

You can reach the Pullman district by Metra train line or by car. Begin your visit at the **Historic Pullman Foundation and Visitor's Center** at 11111 South Forestville Avenue, where you can learn the history of this unique community and join up with a guided tour on the first Sunday of every month, May through October. If you are on your own, purchase a walking-tour map and proceed through the neighborhood.

What you'll see are the preserved remains of well-planned row houses arranged in hierarchical detail according to the rank of their residents in the Pullman employee chain. The Hotel Florence, a Queen Anne-style building that dates back to 1881, recently underwent a lavish restoration; its Sunday brunch is a lovely occasion. The **Pullman Porter Museum**, at 10406 South Maryland Avenue, is Chicago's first African American labor history museum, paying tribute to the first president of the

Brotherhood of Sleeping Car Porters and to the African American railroad attendants. The museum has a collection of vintage historical photos as well as a model train exhibit.

EXCURSIONS

To the North

The city's northern suburbs are affluent and beautiful. If you have a car and want to see how the rich and sometimes-famous live, drive up Sheridan Road along the lake through Evanston, Wilmette, and Winnetka, all the way to Lake Forest. These towns have the large homes and idyllic, tree-lined roads that attract filmmakers who think this posh lifestyle actually represents middle America. Upscale shopping and elegant parks and forest preserves mix with galleries, museums, and schools (Northwestern University has its campus along the lake in Evanston) throughout Chicago's "North Shore."

Ravinia Park

In the town of Highland Park, about 25 miles north of downtown Chicago, the **Ravinia Festival** is a Chicagoland rite of passage. For music under the stars, the festival's outdoor summer concerts at **Ravinia Park** from June through September are hard to beat. Ravinia is summer home to the Chicago Symphony Orchestra, but classical music is only part of what you'll hear and see here. There's also ballet, jazz, big-name popular performers from Tony Bennett to Ray Charles, salsa, gospel, folk, blues, special performances for kids during the day, and more.

Families, couples, and large groups of friends come a few hours ahead of evening performance time and set out picnic dinners complete with candelabras and fine wines, but you can just buy something here (everything from snacks to gourmet meals), spread out a blanket, look at the stars, and listen. Lawn admission is $8 for adults, or you can purchase seats in the park's main pavilion that rings the stage. For a Ravinia experience, sit on the lawn. You won't necessarily see the performers on stage, but you'll hear them through the park's elaborate sound system, and you'll have a wonderful view of the stars through the trees. You can get to Ravinia via the Metra train line's Ravinia Special, or on a Ravinia bus that makes several stops in the Loop and at several downtown hotels.

Beautiful Gardens

Just south of Ravinia Park, in the town of Glencoe, is the **Chicago Botanic Garden**: about 300 acres (120 hectares) of lush gardens, rolling hills, representative prairie landscapes, water lilies blooming in an aquatic garden, waterfalls, and miles of walking trails where you can relax and smell the roses. The tranquil Japanese garden of three islands is the favored spot for

The vast, beautiful Chicago Botanic Garden is worth the short excursion to Glencoe.

The Bahá'í House of Worship is interesting to visitors of all nationalities and religions.

many locals; the new greenhouse biodomes promise tropical gardens, rainforests, and arid deserts in every season. If flowers and groomed gardens appeal to you, then this facility—run by the Chicago Horticultural Society—is worth the trip. Plan to spend the day, and be sure to wear your walking shoes. The garden is free, but there is a fee for parking.

A Serene Temple

Overlooking Lake Michigan on Sheridan Road in Wilmette, the **Bahá'í House of Worship** is a destination point for people from all over the world. The Bahá'í religion has its origins in 19th-century Iran (Persia), which are explained in exhibits at the site, but you don't need a guide to enjoy the architectural intricacies in this gleaming white, nine-sided building that incorporates architectural styles and symbols from many of the world's religions. The temple is situated in carefully tended gardens across the road from a park and marina along the lake. Admission is free.

Going West

Oak Park's Architectural Treasures

Just beyond the city's western borders in the historic suburb of **Oak Park**, you'll find a treasury of buildings created by renowned architect **Frank Lloyd Wright**. Wright came to Chicago as a student of Louis Sullivan not long after the Great Chicago Fire and broke away from the master with his own unique "Prairie Style" that mirrored the flat, simple landscape of the Midwest.

Begin your visit at the Oak Park Visitors' Center (158 North Forest Avenue), where you can purchase tickets to the area's architectural and other attractions, make tour reservations, and find out about the town.

Wright lived and worked in the **Frank Lloyd Wright Home and Studio** (951 Chicago Avenue) for two decades, until he ran off to Germany with the wife of a client. A tour of the studio gives a fascinating up-close glimpse of all the details that have made his work so intriguing. For a few dollars you can take a guided tour of the home and studio, or you can wander on your own.

If architecture is your passion, you'll want to see Wright's **Moore House**, one block away at 333 North Forest Avenue, and perhaps tour the town's Historic District, where you'll see homes designed by Wright and several of his disciples. Come in the spring when the flowers are blooming, and take the area tour that begins at the Wright Home and Studio's bookshop.

Oak Park is also the birthplace of author Ernest Hemingway, and although he shunned his boyhood home as a place with wide lawns and narrow minds, the town has nevertheless turned the house into a shrine of sorts. The **Hemingway Birthplace** is at 339 North Oak Park Avenue, just up the block from the **Hemingway Museum**, which is housed in a former church at 200 North Oak Park Avenue.

You can reach Oak Park quickly from downtown Chicago via public transportation on the CTA's Green Line or the Metra commuter train. For drivers, it is only a short drive west on the Eisenhower Expressway.

WHAT TO DO

You can do just about anything in Chicago: shop, stroll, take a tour, study architecture, eat, bike, in-line skate, ice skate, see a symphony or an opera, go to a comedy club, cheer for the Bulls, dance until dawn, sing the blues... You name it, it's here.

ENTERTAINMENT

Music, theater, dance, and improvisational comedy are the mainstays of Chicago nightlife. There is almost too much on offer: you can see a show, then catch some jazz, and finally have a nightcap in your hotel lounge to end the evening.

Classical Music, Opera, and Dance

World-famous Orchestra Hall and Symphony Center, at 220 South Michigan Avenue, is a mainstay for music of many kinds. It is home to the Chicago Symphony Orchestra, but you can also come here for chamber music and solo recitals given by visiting international artists (Tel. 312/294-3000). The Civic Opera House is home to the spectacular Lyric Opera of Chicago and hosts many fine shows. You can also see operatic performances at the Chicago Opera Theatre.

During summer months you can hear music at the Ravinia Festival in the northern suburb of Highland Park, and at the Grant Park Music Festival. For information on current classical concerts and operas, contact the Chicago Music Alliance (Tel. 312/987-1123).

You can also see a wide variety of classic and modern dance in Chicago, from the city's own critically acclaimed classical ballet company, Ballet Chicago, to the modern Hubbard Street Dance Chicago and the River North Dance Company. For information on current and upcoming performances, call the Chicago Dance Coalition Hotline (Tel. 312/419-8383).

Jazz, Blues, and Reggae

The best places for jazz and blues on the North Side are in Old Town and River North. You can' go wrong if you follow your ears into a club along Lincoln Avenue, Clark Street, or Halsted Street. The city's top jazz review is at Jazz Showcase (59 West Grand Avenue) in River North, a split-level club that is always crowded and attracts such big names as Wynton Marsalis and Dexter Gordon. Andy's Jazz Club, a downscale place at 11 East Hubbard Street, is popular with jazz-lovers who say they go to hear the music, not watch the people. The jazz is authentic here, and the joint starts jump-

Opportunities to attend classical music events are many: here, the renowned Chicago Symphony Orchestra.

ing right after work. In the Loop, Hothouse (31 East Balbo Street) is a center for international jazz performers; it books a variety of jazz, blues, and mambo bands.

For a nightly scene that's been around since the days of Al Capone, check out The Green Mill Cocktail Lounge on the corner of North Broadway and West Lawrence. For some-place new and grand, try the 1940s-style Green Dolphin Street club at 2200 North Ashland Avenue. Jazz in Chicago got its start on the South Side, where the Cotton Club (1710 South Michigan Avenue) always has room for more music-lovers.

Blues can be heard wailing most nights from Kingston Mines (2548 North Halsted Street) and B.L.U.E.S. (2519 North Halsted Street) in Lincoln Park; at Blue Chicago (736 North Clark Street) in River North; and at Buddy Guy's Legends on the near South Side (754 South Wabash Street). For Jamaican reggae music, don't miss The Wild Hare and Singing Armadillo Factory at 3530 North Clark Street.

Most places have cover charges (entry fees), and it's rec-ommended that you call ahead to find out exactly who is playing and what time the shows start.

Folk Music, Nightclubs, and Rock

There are a variety of places on the North Side where the young and hip congregate to dance, hear music, and occasion-

Free Concerts Every Wednesday

Classical music lovers: Stop in at the Chicago Cultural Center (downtown on Michigan Avenue between Randolph and Washington streets) to hear a free miniconcert any Wednesday afternoon at 12:15pm, upstairs in Preston Bradley Hall. Take a look at the Tiffany mosaics on the wall and ceiling while you're there.

Chicago is a founding center of jazz and blues, and this club, Buddy Guy's Legends, upholds the tradition.

ally admire each other's body piercings. The Abbey Pub (3420 West Grace Street) is a modest place with live Irish music and other folk acts. Schubas Tavern (3159 North Southport Avenue) is a great place to see top-rate entertainers in an intimate environment. The Old Town School of Folk Music (909 West Armitage Avenue) features an eclectic blend of entertainment, rather tame by today's standards, but carrying on the tradition of Chicago's folk boom of the 1950s, 60s, and 70s.

Alternative rock and youth are the scene at Lounge Ax (2438 Lincoln Avenue), Metro (3730 North Clark Street), and Crobar (1543 North Kingsbury Street). For far-out, check out Neo in Lincoln Park (2350 North Clark Street), a large club where you'll hear funk and New Wave dance tracks, Red Dog in Wicker Park (1958 West North Avenue), and the Liar's Club dance club (1665 West Fullerton), a spot that bridges the clean-cut and the cutting-edge.

Theater

Chicago is home to a vital, vast, and varied community of regional theatrical companies. Countless Hollywood film and TV stars began their careers on the stages of tiny theaters on Chicago's North Side. Many shows produced here later move to New York as award-winning Broadway and off-Broadway productions. But you can also see some of the hottest Broadway productions on tour at the big Loop theaters.

While scores of theaters are spread throughout the city, there are a few distinct theater districts in Chicago. One is in Old Town, where the Steppenwolf Theatre Company and the Royal George Theatre stage impressive theatrical events and many original works. Lincoln Park, Lakeview, and Southport also boast their share of fine theater companies. The city has

The James R. Thompson Center Halloween Festival is one of many in Chicago that draws crowds each year.

recently been promoting the North Loop Theater District, prompted by the multimillion-dollar renovation and restoration of several large theaters. On the South Side, the ETA Creative Arts Foundation (Tel. 773/752-3955) is a lively performing arts center, as is the Court Theater on the campus of the University of Chicago (Tel. 773/753-4472).

The League of Chicago Theatres provides up-to-date performance information of its member theaters (Tel. 900-225-2225; call is $1 per minute). You might also want to pick up the latest issues of Chicago's free weekly newspapers, the *Chicago Reader* and *New City,* for their comprehensive listings and reviews.

Lakefront Summer Festivals

The city sponsors the following events in or near Grant Park, some of which last four days or more. Time your trip for these Chicago highlights and experience the festivities that attract locals by the hundreds of thousands. Contact the Mayor's Office of Special Events (Tel. 312/744-3315; website www.ci.chi.il.us/tourism) for exact dates.

Chicago Blues Festival: First weekend in June.

Chicago Gospel Festival: Mid-June.

Taste of Chicago: Food booths from the city's famous restaurants; end of June through 4 July.

Chicago Country Music Festival: Last weekend in June.

Venetian Night: Boat parade held in the harbor off Grant Park and the Museum Campus; last weekend in July.

Chicago Air and Water Show: Sea and sky show off the shores of Lake Michigan; late August.

"Viva! Chicago": Latin music festival; end of August.

Chicago Jazz Festival: First weekend of September.

Celtic Fest Chicago: Mid-September.

Chicago's beaches offer placid water for swimming and a lake-front view.

In person, you can visit HotTix Box Offices (Tel. 888-225-8844, toll-free) throughout the city to purchase half-price tickets for same-day performances at more than 125 area theaters; there is a HotTix office inside the Visitor Center across the street from the Water Tower on Michigan Avenue at Chicago Avenue.

SPORTS AND RECREATION

Although it's known for harsh weather, Chicago has many months of blissful breezes and moderate temperatures, when it seems just about everybody heads to the lakeshore for fresh air and fun. But you can head away from the lake for a wide variety of activities in Chicago's parks, forest preserves, and golf courses. And don't forget the city's five major professional sports teams—there's bound to be a game during your stay whatever the time of year.

Parks

Chicago has an elaborate park system, 29 miles (47 km) of lakeshore coast, running paths, fishing piers, and eight yacht harbors. The public availability of the waterfront makes Chicago unique among major US cities. The Chicago Park District (Tel. 312/747-2200; TTY 312/986-0726) operates and maintains 500 parks offering a wide range of athletic and recreational activities. Dozens of tennis courts and golf courses are enjoyed by residents and visitors alike for a nominal fee. Also, two world-renowned conservatories (Lincoln Park Conservatory on the North Side and Garfield Park Conservatory on the West Side) blossom with year-'round flower shows.

> There's an intense rivalry between the Chicago Cubs and Chicago White Sox baseball teams. It's a North Side/South Side thing. Sox fans say C-U-B stands for "Can't Understand Baseball." What do Cubs fans say about the Sox fans? It's mostly unprintable.

The city boasts more than 500 baseball diamonds, 500 basketball courts, 200 football/soccer fields, 6 public golf courses, 2 swimming lagoons, 9 harbors, 75 soccer fields, 56 outdoor swimming pools, and almost 700 tennis courts.

Beaches

Public beaches run along Lake Michigan from Oak Street Beach up to Hollywood Avenue. The beaches are free, and lifeguards are on duty throughout the summer season. The water is generally cold until mid-July, but the gently sloping shoreline and almost complete lack of tides and waves provide safe swimming even for toddlers. The names of the beaches coincide with the major east-west cross-streets that lead to the waterfront.

If you're young and shapely (or simply like to be around the best young bodies), definitely check out Oak Street Beach. If you want to mingle, bring a volleyball and go to North Avenue Beach, just a few blocks north. Belmont Harbor has boats and rocks, not beaches, and this is a favorite place for uptown gay men, who lounge around on Sunday afternoons with the newspaper. Just a few blocks north, near Addison Street, is the so-called doggie beach, where locals bring their beloved canines to an impromptu "play group" and have been known to find friendship and even romance. Farther north, Foster Beach is a place for families, and Hollywood Beach is a popular gay beach.

Biking, Jogging, and Skating

The best place to walk, jog, in-line skate, or bike is along the Lakefront Trail, which offers miles of beautiful paved pathway from downtown to the north as well as south. The city has more than 18 miles of bike paths here and in Grant Park. You can rent a bike or find information on group bike tours at Bike Chicago on Navy Pier (Tel. 312/944-2337) or at the Bike Stop at 1034 West Belmont Avenue in Lake View (Tel. 773/868-6800).

In winter months the city sponsors Skate on State, a free ice-skating rink in the heart of downtown Chicago, located on State Street between Washington and Randolph. You can skate outdoors under the Ferris wheel on Navy Pier, and there's a beautiful public rink at the north end of Grant Park.

Boat Rides

With so much water within and around the city, Chicago naturally has a variety of boat tours and entertainment cruises along the Chicago River and in Lake Michigan. Wendella Sightseeing Boats (Tel. 312/337-1446) and Mercury Chicago Skyline Cruises (Tel. 312/332-1353) operate from April

*The young and beautiful come out to play at the edge of
Oak Street Beach.*

through October and are very popular. From Navy Pier you
can choose from several entertainment cruise ships year
'round. Try the Odyssey (Tel. 630/990-0800) or the Spirit of
Chicago (Tel. 312/836-7899).

Golf

Golfing in Chicago is plentiful, although not necessarily chal-
lenging. For wonderful views of lake and city, try the city's 9-
hole lakefront Sydney R. Marovitz Course (commonly known
as Waveland) in Lincoln Park. Practice your swing nearby at
the Diversey Driving Range. Or avoid the crowds and go south
to the South Lake Shore Drive Course at 71st Street. The Jackson Park Golf Course is a bit out of the way, but it's the Chica-

go Park District's only 19-hole course. Club rentals are available at city-run courses.

For general information on the city's golf courses, call the Chicago Park District (Tel. 312/747-2623) during normal business hours. You can also try the MetroGolf Illinois Center (Tel. 312/616-1234) between Columbus Drive and Lake Shore Drive, near the river.

Spectator Sports

Chicago loves its sports teams. The Bulls, the Cubs, the White Sox, the Bears, the Blackhawks, the Wolves—any season is the right season for sports in the Windy City. To get tickets to a sporting event, call or visit the individual stadiums, or call Ticketmaster (Tel. 312/559-1212).

Basketball

The Chicago Bulls, six-time National Basketball Association champions, play at the new United Center on West Madison Street. Michael Jordan has retired, but the Bulls should still be popular because, win or lose, Chicagoans have a passion for basketball. For Bulls tickets and schedule information call (312) 559-1212.

Baseball

Nothing demonstrates the local sports fans' loyalty more than the crowded stands at Wrigley Field, where the Chicago Cubs baseball team hasn't won a World Series since 1908. It might be Wrigley Field's ivy walls and intimate atmosphere that keep fans filling the place. Whatever it is, a day game at Wrigley Field on the city's North Side is a quintessential Chicago experience. Call (312) 321-2827 for Cubs tickets and schedule information.

Of course, that's not what the rival White Sox baseball team fans will tell you. The Sox, who last took the championship title in 1917, have shiny new Comiskey Park on the South Side, with one of the best ballpark food courts going. Call (312) 321-1769 for White Sox tickets and schedule information.

Football

When it comes to championships, the Chicago Bears football team holds its own. They won the 1986 Super Bowl, and although they've fallen on tough times, the fans still believe in them. See the Bears at Soldier Field at the south end of Grant Park. Call (847) 615-2327 for Bears tickets and schedule information.

Hockey

Hockey is as popular as the city's other spectator sports; the fans work themselves up into a tizzy watching the Chicago Blackhawks, the National Hockey League team, play at the United Center. You can also see the Chicago Wolves International Hockey League team at the Rosemont Horizon in suburban Rosemont. For Blackhawks tickets and information call (312) 455-4500; for Wolves information call (312) 559-1212.

NEIGHBORHOOD TOURS

The city's Office of Tourism sponsors weekly neighborhood tours showcasing individual Chicago neighborhoods. The Chicago Neighborhood Tours are on Saturdays, beginning at the Chicago Cultural Center (where buses take you to each four-hour tour's starting point), and travel into more than 15 neighborhoods on the city's South, North, and West sides on a rotating basis. Call (312) 742-1190 for information and reservations, as well as dates for special tours.

You might also enjoy a narrated sightseeing tour aboard buses belonging to the city's two popular tour companies. The Chicago Trolley Company (Tel. 312/663-0260) offers an all-day pass with unlimited drop-offs and pick-ups on its red-

and-green trolley-style buses. The Chicago Motor Coach (Tel. 312/922-8919) features red double-decker buses that offer similar but somewhat more limited all-day service to the city's cultural and sightseeing highlights.

For a quirky tour, try the Chicago Supernatural Ghost Tours (Tel. 708/499-0300) or the Untouchable Gangster Tours (Tel. 773/881-1195). Call ahead for tour times and reservations.

SHOPPING

Chicago offers some of the finest shopping in the country. The "Magnificent Mile," a one-mile strip along North Michigan Avenue from Oak Street south to the Chicago River, has three vertical shopping malls with more than 200 shops and restaurants. Chicago Place, at 700 North Michigan Avenue, anchored by Saks Fifth Avenue, houses Talbots, Louis Vuitton, and Ann Taylor. The 900 North Michigan Shops, a six-story vertical emporium, includes Bloomingdale's and Gucci among its flagship stores. Water Tower Place, home to Chicago-based Marshall Field and Company, also has Lord & Taylor and many other top-name stores and specialty boutiques. Oak Street itself is a veritable "Who's Who" of upscale smaller stars, including Gianni Versace, Giorgio Armani, Barney's, and Jil Sander, to

Frango, Anyone?

When in Chicago, pass up Godiva and head straight for the Frango Mints sold in the food department at Marshall Field's. Created in the 1920s, the unassuming little candies are a quintessential Chicago treat and make a great souvenir or hostess gift. These beloved chocolate mints are made right at the store's confectionery on State Street and have morphed into a million-dollar business—and you can only get them here. Try the originals in the green box, and take a box home for your friends, too!

name just a few. Stroll south along the Magnificent Mile and you'll see Niketown, Crate & Barrel, Bigsby & Kruthers, Neiman Marcus, Mark Shale, Victoria's Secret, Elizabeth Arden, Pottery Barn, Tiffany, Cartier, and many more upscale stores.

American Girl Place, on East Chicago just off Michigan Avenue, is the first store of its kind in the world, completely devoted to the doll-and-book marketing concept that is popular with young girls. The Chicago Store in the Tribune Tower near the river features unique items such as city surplus and salvage, memorabilia, quality souvenirs, and selected gift items from the shops of the city's museums and cultural organizations.

Shopaholics can amuse themselves for days along the Magnificent Mile.

Farther south, at the corner of State and Randolph streets in the Loop, sits the grande dame of American department stores. The original site of the first Marshall Field's department store (opened in 1852) is now an 11-story, 450-department extravaganza, boasting a glorious Tiffany dome and seven wonderful places to eat. On the next block south, the Carson, Pirie, Scott Company (1 South State Street) is another fine department store with a long history in Chicago as well as a landmark building designed by Louis Sullivan. Both stores install wonderful holiday windows in December each year.

When shopping in Chicago, don't limit yourself to Loop and Michigan Avenue stores. You'll find retail stores and ethnic specialty shops all over the city. The River North Gallery District has some 60 art galleries within a one mile radius from the intersection of Superior and Franklin streets. Antiques can be found in the North Side neighborhoods; try the Antique Mall of Wrigleyville at 3336 North Clark Street or the enormous Chicago Antique Mall at 3045 North Lincoln Avenue.

ARCHITECTURE

Perhaps Chicago's most identifiable claim to fame is its architectural tradition. Chicago is the birthplace of the skyscraper, and its architects have initiated international architectural styles and movements, the most notable being the Chicago School and the Prairie School. The city is a living museum of famous buildings, thanks to the genius of men such as city-planner Daniel Burnham, Louis Sullivan, Frank Lloyd Wright, Ludwig Mies van der Rohe, Helmut Jahn, and hundreds of others.

Early architectural marvels of the city include the 1886 Rookery Building (209 South LaSalle Street), the Chicago Cultural Center (at the corner of Randolph Street and South Michigan Avenue), and the Chicago Board of Trade Building (141 West Jackson Street).

The Chicago Architecture Foundation (Tel. 312/922-8687), at 224 South Michigan Avenue, offers more than 60 city tours, including a Chicago landmarks tour, a tour focusing on early and modern skyscrapers, a riverboat tour, a tour of the city's buildings on the National Register of Historic Places, the Frank Lloyd Wright Robie House in Hyde Park, the Prairie Avenue Historic District, and more.

Chicago Athenaeum: The Museum of Architecture and Design (6 North Michigan Avenue; Tel. 312/251-0175) is an international museum of art, architecture, and design.

If you are interested in one of the true masters of modern American architecture, consider a day-trip to the adjacent western suburb of Oak Park (see page 78), where you can witness Frank Lloyd Wright's mastery of building design and space in the Frank Lloyd Wright Historic District and take a tour of his home and studio. Contact the Oak Park Visitors' Center at (708) 848-1500.

ACTIVITIES FOR CHILDREN

Chicago is a great place to take the kids. A top spot for families is the Lincoln Park Zoo, where little ones particularly enjoy the Farm in the Zoo and the many hands-on activities at the indoor-outdoor Pritzker Children's Zoo. Navy Pier and the Chicago Children's Museum are a natural destination for families, but don't underestimate the hours of enjoyment you can pack in at the Field Museum and Shedd Aquarium. These two Museum

The Unity Temple (1908) is one of Frank Lloyd Wright's landmark Prairie-style projects.

Lincoln Park Zoo is the favored diversion of many visiting (and local) children.

Campus highlights are excellent destinations for families, offering a great range of activities for everyone. At the Field Museum, don't miss the Dinosaur Hall and the Ancient Egypt exhibits, as well as the Crown Family Place for Wonder on the main level, which is a great hands-on exploratorium for little ones.

The Art Institute of Chicago has a special place for children on the lower level. The DuSable Museum of African American History has an extensive summer program for children. And the Museum of Science and Industry is a natural: plan to spend the day here if you have curious children who love to explore.

Perhaps less obvious but nevertheless enjoyable family destinations include Southport Lanes (3325 North Southport Avenue) for bowling, Skate on State for winter fun, the Harold Washington Library Center's second-floor children's library (with many special programs), and the Spertus Museum (618 South Michigan Avenue), where kids can participate in a hands-on simulated archeological dig. There are special children's matinee performances at Orchestra Hall, kid's craft activities at the Museum of Contemporary Art, and a family performance series at the ETA Creative Arts Foundation.

Naturally, kids who don't fear heights enjoy the view from atop the John Hancock Center and the Sears Tower Skydeck.

EATING OUT

Variety is the key to Chicago's dining scene, not only in types of cuisine but in pricing and ambiance as well. In this metropolis you can fine dine with crystal, china, and a world-class wine—or put on your sandals and get a great dish of *pad thai* for a few dollars.

Chicagoans enjoy eating out *à deux*, or en masse, but with so many business travelers and singles in the city, dining out solo is not unusual either. Because the workday begins early (traders start at 7:30am), the city has its popular breakfast spots, and the bottomless coffee cup has caught on in many establishments. A hot little-known favorite of the Loop early-bird crowd is Heaven on Seven, where delicious Cajun/Creole food is served for breakfast and lunch in an informal atmosphere. Yes, in Chicago there is a place where you can get banana-pecan French toast—a Creole specialty—for breakfast in a hurry! You can enjoy a relaxing Sunday brunch at many top-notch eateries for a fraction of the dinner price.

There are more than 6,000 restaurants in the Windy City. While it is home to the world's busiest McDonald's restaurant (the 24-hour Rock 'n' Roll McDonald's in River North), Chicago is also known for magnificent steak houses and fine French

---

"A Taste of Chicago"

Probably the best way to sample the city's cuisine is to visit during the first week of July, when this city-sponsored lakefront festival brings out the top eateries. Each participating restaurant has a booth where you can sample everything from deep-dish pizza to gourmet appetizers, cheesecake to ice cream. This is the country's largest outdoor food festival, attracting about 3 million visitors every year. And the prices are affordable. Come for lunch and eat your way right into dinner.

and Italian cuisine, with some restaurants ranked among the very best in the US. Maybe it's something about the heartland, where the livestock is fed from Great Plains corn and the produce is grown in the country's farm belt. But Chicago offers virtually any kind of food you can imagine.

Competition for the city's dining money has led many inventive restaurateurs to put service, price, and atmosphere on the menu of what matters most, right up there along with the quality of the food itself. Entrepreneurs such as Rich Melman of "Lettuce Entertain You, Inc." have created spectacular specialty eateries with big design and big flavor, while world-class chefs the likes of Charlie Trotter and Jean Joho have opened their own restaurants in Chicago to tremendous success.

Chicago's Rock n' Roll McDonald's is the busiest branch in the United States.

If you are invited to a "Lettuce Entertain You" restaurant, be sure to wear something chic and be prepared to wait: the length of the wait is often more shocking than the cost of your meal in a place like Scoozi!, but the people-watching is always splendid. In most places you can purchase a drink and hors d'oeuvres at the bar while you're waiting, and some restaurants even offer a complimentary glass of wine to would-be diners.

If it's see-and-be-seen you're after, Chicago has plenty of places to do just that in the West Loop. Flocking to the trendiest restaurants is a popular hobby among young urban professionals, and there are plenty of cellular phones and leather jackets in the top places, adding a little high-tech glitter to your dinner along with some pretty impressive state-of-the-moment cuisine concoctions. While dinner hour starts as early as 5pm in Chicago, the wait on weekends at the most popular establishments can push your dinner time past 10pm. We recommend reservations if the restaurant offers that service.

Tables with a View

No matter how good-looking or well dressed your fellow diners might be, don't forget about the wonderful views the city's landscape can provide. With three of the world's tallest buildings and a shimmering lake at its feet, Chicago has many restaurants that offer spectacular views along with your entrées.

Bill and Hillary Clinton reportedly enjoy the waterfront view at Riva on Navy Pier, but many power-brokers prefer the

The pizza named after the city itself — you can't visit Chicago without trying "Chicago-style" pizza.

City of 6,000 eateries: you're guaranteed to find a meal that suits your taste in Chicago.

skytop views from Everest or the waterfront and skyline views from the 70th floor location of Cité. Be sure to call in advance if a table by the window is your heart's desire.

Celebrity-owned restaurants are also part of the eating experience here. It seems just about every sports superstar has had his own place at one time or another. Today it's Harry Caray's and Michael Jordan's that are pulling in the crowds. Don't expect great food in these places (and don't expect to see Michael either, except on rare occasions), although a nice hamburger or well-turned pork chop is sometimes served alongside some really good mashed potatoes.

Fine Finger Foods

Some clichés about Chicago's eateries do hold true: barbe-cued ribs and deep-dish pizza come to mind immediately because they really are done so well here. Is it simply a coincidence that the most popular convenience foods in Chicago—deep-dish pizza, ribs, Italian beef, red hots—are eaten with your fingers? Or is it because, in the "City that Works," filling up quickly with a hearty meal was long a goal of area eateries?

You won't be in Chicago long before someone will proudly point you in the direction of one of the city's top pizza restaurants and command, "Try it, you'll like it!" Most people do. The world of flat-dough pizza has never been the same since this flaky-dough creation which is twice as thick (and twice as good, some will swear) was invented in 1943 at the original Pizzeria Uno. There's no tossing of pizza crusts in these establishments: the dough is flaky and deep, filled like an actual pie with sauce, cheese, and other delicious additions. Chicagoans are pretty proud of this creation, and will argue at length over the merits of the versions of this dish served at different local restaurants.

Italian beef, a combination of extra-thin slices of meat topped with peppers, onions, and spices, is served almost everywhere red hots are sold. To get a real taste, avoid the greasy spoons and head for Al's No.1 Italian Beef (1079

"Pop and a Red Hot—Hold the Onions!"

While much of the world orders Coke, Pepsi, and Orange Crush either by brand name or by the generic word "soda," people native to Chicagoland invariably will ask for a "pop," often accompanied by a request for a "red hot." Here a hot dog or frankfurter is known as a red hot. Order a red hot with "the works" and you'll get raw onion, a slice of sour pickle, tomato, hot peppers, and mustard. Hot dog vendors, by the way, don't usually have sauerkraut (and if they do, it's cold!).

West Taylor Street) in Little Italy. Spare ribs are served to perfection at the three locations of Carson's Ribs, where takeout is big business and side dishes are as good as the main event.

At Chicago's many German restaurants, it's a tradition to stuff yourself at lunch with a hefty sandwich or sauerbraten and a mug of brew.

Authentic Ethnic Eateries

Ethnic food is part of the eating experience in Chicago, popular for the variety of foods you can try and for reasonable prices in relatively casual settings. Forget about "fusion." You'll find plenty of places to find an honest Old World meal in the city, especially in the homey neighborhoods of Greektown, Chinatown, German Town, Andersonville, and Pilsen.

Go north to West Devon Avenue and choose from among the best Indian restaurants in the city, tucked among sari shops and Pakistani grocery stores. The curry dishes and *naan* bread fill the air with the scent of another world. The city's best Vietnamese restaurants are also found a little out of the way—but well worth the ride—on North Broadway.

The neighborhood of Andersonville (on Clark Street, about 5200 North) is the city's "Little Sweden." Here you'll

---

Regular Coffee and a Bagel

Starbucks may be everywhere, but it's the coffee and baked goods at the Corner Bakery (a local chain that began as a River North shop at Clark Street and North Avenue) that have Chicago's heart. If you order it "regular," you'll get coffee with milk and sugar. Order it "light" and you'll get a funny look. If you want extra milk, just say so!

For a change of pace, grab a "regular" coffee and a pastry and while away the afternoon in a quiet Chicago café.

find authentic Swedish meatballs and wonderful cinnamon rolls on the menu. Farther from the lake, visit Lincoln Square (where North Lincoln Avenue, Western Avenue, and Lawrence Street converge) and find yourself in German Town, where you can sample some of the best sauerbraten, schnitzel, and *spaetzel* in the Midwest.

Pilsen attracts visitors to the Mexican Fine Arts Museum Center. So when you're in the area, you should also stop at one of the authentic, family-run neighborhood restaurants serving Mexican food the way it has been cooked for generations.

And don't forget Greektown, Little Italy, and Chinatown (discussed in the "Where to Go" section of this guide), which are loaded with restaurants that cater to folks who have big appetites for moderately priced, authentically ethnic food and local color.

INDEX

HANDY TRAVEL TIPS

An A–Z Summary of Practical Information

A

ACCOMMODATIONS

The average cost of a downtown Chicago hotel room is $115 for a standard room for two. Suites and luxury accommodations can run in excess of $500 daily. With more than 25,000 hotel and motel rooms in the city and an average occupancy rate of 86 percent, it's generally easy to book a room, unless the city is overrun by one of its many large conventions.

Where to stay. Most people who visit the city for pleasure stay in or close to the downtown area, although there are some motels and motor lodges in the city's surrounding neighborhoods, and many business travelers stay near the airport. The listings below focus on the downtown and Near North neighborhoods.

Reservations. Call in advance to guarantee availability and rates. Generally a credit card is taken to guarantee your reservation. Ask if there is a cancellation penalty, as some facilities will charge for rooms reserved but not used. Call the Illinois Reservation Service (Tel. 800-491-1800, toll-free) for assistance with reservations. The Illinois Bureau of Tourism (Tel. 800-2-CONNECT, toll-free) is very helpful with accommodation recommendations.

Hotels. The city's largest hotels are the Hyatt Regency Chicago (2,019 rooms); the Palmer House Hilton (1,639 rooms); Chicago Hilton and Towers (1,543 rooms); Sheraton Hotel and Towers (1,200 rooms); and Chicago Marriott Hotel (1,172 rooms). The top hotels offer a variety of guest services and amenities, often including a fitness room or visiting privileges to a nearby sports club/gym; swimming pool; and housekeeping and personal services such as shoeshine, garment press, and computer/fax services.

There are several "five-star" hotels in Chicago. To obtain this status, the facility must have an on-site restaurant and offer a full spectrum of guest services and beautiful appointments throughout the hotel.

If you drive or rent a car, check on parking availability, as many hotels require guests to pay a nightly parking fee.

Chicago

Motor lodges and motels. Smaller rooms, more affordable rates, and parking spots are offered at motor lodges, which are generally outside the Loop.

Bed-and-breakfast inns. In the last few years this home-away-from-home business has finally expanded in Chicago to include rooms in old graystones and complete apartments downtown. Prices will run you a bit less than at many hotels, with a minimum two-night stay in most accommodations. To book a room, contact Bed and Breakfast Chicago (Tel. 312/591-0085; fax 312/649-9243).

AIRPORTS

There are two major airports in Chicago: O'Hare International Airport and Midway Airport. Both airports provide a variety of transfer options to the downtown area, with taxis to the Loop for a fare ranging from $20 to $30. Commercial vans and buses as well as public transportation are also available from both airports to the Loop and Near North areas, and many of the finer hotels provide courtesy shuttle buses.

O'Hare International Airport. Located in the northwest corner of the city, O'Hare is approximately 30 to 50 minutes from downtown Chicago, depending on traffic and mode of transportation. It is the commercial aviation capital of the world and the hub of national air transportation in the US, handling more passengers and aircraft operations than any other airport in the world. Approximately 180,000 travelers pass through O'Hare each day. The total airport complex covers nearly 7,700 acres (3,115 hectares) with 162 aircraft gates housed in four terminal buildings. O'Hare has 50 commercial, commuter, and cargo airlines offering frequent service to virtually any destination in the world.

Getting to O'Hare via CTA: The CTA Blue Line train provides 24-hour service between downtown Chicago and O'Hare International Airport. Lower-level pedestrian passageways inside the airport terminals lead directly to the CTA station. The station is equipped with an elevator to take passengers with mobility impairments to and from the platform. For additional information, call (312) 836-7000 (TTY 312/836-4949).

CTA Special Services: Door-to-door, lift-equipped transportation is available to and from O'Hare to both Chicago-area residents and out-of-town visitors. One week's notice is required for out-of-town users (Tel. 312/917-4357; TTY 312/917-1338)

The Bus/Shuttle Center at O'Hare: Door-to-door vans and shuttle buses provide transfers to downtown Chicago as well as to various locations in the city and suburbs (and even to nearby destinations in Wisconsin and Indiana). The Bus/Shuttle Center is centrally located between Terminals 1, 2, and 3. Follow the overhead signs in the Baggage Claim (lower level) areas of each domestic terminal to the nearest underground Pedestrian Walkway. Proceed to Elevator Centers 3 or 4 and press the Bus/Shuttle Center button.

Midway Airport. On Chicago's South Side, Midway is about 20 minutes from downtown. It is much smaller than O'Hare and therefore more manageable for travelers within the US. It's also closer to the Loop, so taxicab fare is a few dollars cheaper than the ride from O'Hare, about $20. You can also take the CTA Orange Line from the airport to downtown Chicago. For Midway Airport information, call (773) 838-0600.

B

BICYCLE RENTAL/HIRE

The best place to bike is along the Lakefront Trail, which offers miles of beautiful paved pathway. There are plenty of places to lock your bike, which you should definitely do if you plan to leave it even for a minute. Bicycles can be rented at Bike Chicago on Navy Pier (Tel. 312/944-2337; 800-915-2453, toll-free) or at the Bike Stop (1034 West Belmont Avenue; Tel. 773/868-6800) in Lakeview.

BUDGETING for YOUR TRIP

The average hotel room in Chicago costs a bit more than $100 per night. Lunch on the run will cost between $5 and $15, depending on your taste and appetite. Dinner can be purchased for as little as $12, with the sky as the limit. An evening movie ticket in Chicago will run you more than $8.00 (matinees are often cheaper), and a telephone call from a public pay phone currently costs $0.35. To see a live theater production, classical or pop musical performance, or ballet, you might pay up to $65, although desirable seating is often available for considerably less. Rides on buses and "El" trains cost $1.50, although various multiple-ticket plans can make public transportation cheaper the more you ride.

C

CAR RENTAL/HIRE

You might not need or want a car in Chicago unless you are planning to go beyond the boundaries of the Chicago Transportation Authority (CTA) trains and buses. If you do rent a car, you will need a valid driver's license and major credit card, and generally you must be at least 25 years of age. International visitors must secure an International Driving Permit to validate a foreign license. Some of the more popular car rental agencies are:

Alamo Rent-A-Car	(847) 671-7662; (312) 332-2908; 800-327-9633 (toll-free)
Avis Rent A Car	(773) 694-5600; 800-331-1212 (toll-free)
Budget Rent A Car	(773) 686-6800; 800-527-0700 (toll-free)
Dollar Rent A Car	(773) 686-2030; 800-800-4000 (toll-free)
Enterprise Rent-A-Car	(847) 298-3600; 800-325-8007 (toll-free)
Hertz Rent A Car	(773) 686-7272; 800-654-3131 (toll-free)
National Car Rental	(773) 694-4640; 800-227-7368 (toll-free)
Thrifty Car Rental	(847) 928-2000; (773) 582-1049; (312) 781-9900; 800-367-2277 (toll-free)

CLIMATE

True to its reputation, the city gets frigid in winter, and snowstorms can come as late as April. However, the city's climate is also moderated by Lake Michigan. Breezes from the lake warm the city in winter, and the water has a cooling effect during the summer in what is otherwise a landlocked Midwestern state. While many other American cities can be brutal in August, Chicago has the beaches and the breezes to make even a deep-summer visit enjoyable. Local weather reporters often talk of "lake effect" to indicate conditions near Lake Michigan where the water temperature and wind make both summer and winter extremes more moderate.

Despite its blustery reputation as the "Windy City," Chicago actually ranks 14th for wind velocity in the US. Chicago's winters are mostly sunny, with an average of 30 inches of snow from November through March. In spring, expect an average high temperature of 55°F (13°C) and a low of 40°F (4°C), with approximately 11 rainy days in March, April, and May. Weather from June until September is near-perfect for outdoor activities, but expect a few tropically hot days with temperature and humidity both hitting 100°F (38°C). By mid-July and continuing through late September, Lake Michigan is perfect for swimming. The lake's warm waters keep the city temperate throughout the fall, although some early-morning low temperatures can be about 38°F (3°C).

Given the capricious weather forecast for winter months, the best time to visit Chicago for pleasure is May through October, with winter holiday trips an obvious exception.

Chicago's average monthly temperature:

	J	F	M	A	M	J	J	A	S	O	N	D
°F	21	25	37	49	59	69	73	71	64	53	40	27
°C	-6	-4	3	9	15	21	23	22	18	12	4	-3

The city offers an online weather service with current conditions and forecasts: www.ci.chi.il.us/tourism/weather

Chicago

CLOTHING

What to pack will naturally depend upon the time of year you'll be visiting the city. Chinos seem to be the uniform of the day for men of all ages. Women have a bit more versatility and can top their outfit with a sweater twinset to fit in almost anywhere, it seems. In summer bring a swimsuit and sneakers for outdoor excursions and a lightweight jacket for evening. Black being the most basic of colors for the hip and happening, pack black if you're planning to hit the younger, trendier, sleeker parts of town. Rolling up your clothing is one of the best travel packing tips ever: it's compact, and everything comes out of the suitcase wrinkle-free.

Winter is the trickiest season, and that can mean any time from November through March. Vanity does not prevail when the winds are freezing and the snow is thigh-high. Pack gloves, hats, long underwear, and very, very warm waterproof boots. You'll be glad you did!

CRIME and SAFETY

Chicago is a large city, and visitors are advised to exercise the same appropriate cautions they would observe in other urban areas worldwide. Many parts of Chicago experience a high degree of crime. If you are uncomfortable in a neighborhood or an area, leave as soon as possible. Be aware that straying more than a block or two from a certain neighborhood can take you into a high-crime area. This is especially true in the Gold Coast, River North, and Old Town neighborhoods, where tourists (especially drunk ones) are sometimes preyed upon. Don't walk around at night in Hyde Park at all, even on the university campus.

Exercise the following common-sense practices. Avoid dark and deserted streets at night. Do not carry large sums of cash. Instead, make purchases with traveler's checks, personal checks, bank cards, or credit cards. Do not share personal information with strangers. While sightseeing or using public transportation, carry purses and handbags close to your body with the fastener facing the body. Avoid placing purses or briefcases on the backs of chairs or on the floor while dining. Always keep wallets in an inside front pocket; never carry wallets or other valuables in back pockets. Pay attention when making purchases or opening your purse or wallet. Never allow yourself to be distracted. Remain alert at all times, especially in crowded and noisy areas. If you get lost, go to an open business and ask for help.

In an emergency, phone 911 from any phone; there is no charge from coin-operated telephones.

CUSTOMS and ENTRY REGULATIONS

For a stay of less than 90 days, most European nationals who hold a valid ten-year passport and a return ticket on a major airline generally do not need a US visa. Canadian visitors merely need to show proof of nationality. Citizens of Australia, Portugal, and South Africa need a visa, but rules do change, so check with your local US embassy or consulate, or ask your travel agent.

Nonresidents of the US may enter with gifts of up to $100 in value without paying a tax or penalty. Importation of plants, seeds, vegetables, fruits, or other fresh foods is prohibited.

D

DRIVING

Unless you're planning to drive beyond the reach of the CTA's public transportation system, you won't need a car in Chicago. If you drive here, remember that driving is standard throughout the US: drive on the right, pass on the left, stop for red lights. Right turn on red is permitted in Chicago unless a sign indicates otherwise. Downtown, there are quite a few intersections where left turns are prohibited — watch out for the overhead signs that indicate this (the police will get you on this one). Drivers and all passengers must wear seatbelts. Child-safety seats are required for children aged 4 and under.

Gasoline (petrol) is easy to purchase, especially north and west of the immediate downtown and Loop areas.

Parking. Observe parking restrictions and feed the parking meters every day (including Sunday) unless otherwise indicated. Illegally parked cars will be towed by the city and will require a hefty fine to be retrieved from the towing agency (plus you'll pay for the parking ticket itself).

Also beware of those signs in commercial parking lots that say "Parking for customers only. Violators will be towed at owner's expense by Lincoln Towing." These guys mean business! Lookouts with nothing better to do than watch for you to park in the deli lot while you run into the drug store across the street will alert those tow trucks before you can even pay for your cough syrup. It costs more than $100 (and rising) to retrieve your car from them, not to mention the time and aggravation.

Underground parking near Grant Park is one of the better bargains in the city, and it's relatively safe, too. All the garages are run by the Standard Parking Company. For the best rate, choose Monroe Street Underground Parking at Columbus and Monroe, which charges a flat rate of $7 for 24 hours: Monroe Street Underground Parking, Columbus Drive at Monroe Street (Tel. 312/742-7644); Grant Park North Garage, Michigan Avenue at Washington Street (Tel. 312/742-7530); Grant Park South Garage, Michigan Avenue at Van Buren Street (Tel. 312/747-2519).

E

ELECTRICITY

Throughout the United States the standard is 110-volt/60-cycle AC. Plugs have two flat prongs. Overseas visitors without dual-voltage travel appliances will need a transformer and adapter plug for such appliances such as electric razors and hair dryers. These can sometimes be supplied by the housekeeping staff at your hotel, but it's best to travel with your own.

EMBASSIES and CONSULATES

There are more than 60 foreign consulates in Chicago, most located on or near Michigan Avenue.

Australia	No consulate in Chicago, call Washington, DC; Tel. (202) 797-3000
Brazil	401 North Michigan Avenue; Tel. (312) 464-0244
Canada	2 Prudential Plaza, at 180 North Stetson; Tel. (312) 616-1860
France	737 North Michigan Avenue; Tel. (312) 787-5359
Germany	767 North Michigan Avenue; Tel. (312) 580-1199
Greece	650 North St. Clair; Tel. (312) 335-3915
Ireland	400 North Michigan Avenue; Tel. (312) 337-1868
Italy	500 North Michigan Avenue; Tel. (312) 467-1550
Japan	737 North Michigan Avenue; Tel. (312) 280-0400
Mexico	300 North Michigan Avenue; Tel. (312) 855-1380
New Zealand	No consulate in Chicago, call Washington, DC; Tel. (202) 328-4800
South Africa	200 South Michigan Avenue; Tel. (312) 939-7929
Spain	180 North Michigan Avenue; Tel. (312) 782-4588
Switzerland	737 North Michigan Avenue; Tel. (312) 915-0061
Turkey	360 North Michigan Avenue; Tel. (312) 263-0644
UK	400 North Michigan Avenue; Tel. (312) 346-1810

EMERGENCIES
(see also HEALTH AND MEDICAL CARE and POLICE)

Dial 911 from any telephone for emergencies requiring immediate assistance. No coins are required at a pay phone. The operator will note the information and relay it to the police, ambulance, or fire department accordingly.

GAY and LESBIAN TRAVELERS

There is a large gay and lesbian community in the city, primarily in the various North Side neighborhoods. Chicago's Gay and Lesbian

Chicago

Pride Week and accompanying parade held near the end of June are major events. The Gay and Lesbian Pride Week Planning Committee (Tel. 773/348-8243) is a good resource, as is the *Windy City Times*, the city's gay newspaper.

The Gerber/Hart Gay and Lesbian Library and Archives is an additional source of information: 3352 North Paulina Street; Tel. (773) 255-4143; fax (773) 883-3078; email <info@gerberhart.org>.

GETTING THERE

By air. Virtually all major domestic (and most major international) airlines fly into O'Hare International Airport; a smaller number fly to Midway Airport (see Airports). You will have no problems making connections from anywhere in the US. From the UK, Europe, South and Central America, and Asia, the air connections are direct if not nonstop. Beyond the usual first-class, business, and economy fares there are special discount airfares (such as APEX) requiring advance booking and certain restrictions on length of stay. Consult a travel agent or the airlines themselves for further information. Internet airfare discounters are now quite common, as are advertisements in the travel sections of major newspapers.

By car. As the saying goes, "All roads lead to Chicago." The following roads are among the major highways leading into the city:

Interstate 90 connects Chicago with the east and west coasts of the US. From the east, it crosses Indiana into Illinois (including that portion called the "Chicago Skyway"), where it joins Interstate 94 to become first the Dan Ryan Expressway and then the John F. Kennedy Expressway. Eventually, it crosses into Wisconsin on its way to Minnesota and points west.

Interstate 55 (the Adlai E. Stevenson Expressway) leads into the city from the southwest.

Interstate 294 (the Tri-State Tollway) runs north–south about 15 miles (24 km) west of downtown Chicago.

US Highway 41 follows the lakeshore and runs right through the city, where it is known as Lake Shore Drive. It leads north through Wisconsin and on to the upper peninsula of the state of Michigan.

By train or bus. Chicago can be reached from almost anywhere in the US by train and by bus. From the suburbs surrounding Chicago, try Metra (Tel. 312/322-6777), the commuter rail service, or Pace (Tel. 847/364-7223), the commuter bus service.

From places farther afield, Chicago is a major destination for Amtrak trains (Tel. 800-USA-RAIL, toll-free) and Greyhound buses (Tel. 800-231-2222, toll-free). Amtrak trains arrive at Union Station, on the corner of West Adams and Canal streets in the shadow of the Sears Tower and just west of the Chicago River. The Greyhound Bus Station is at 630 West Harrison, not far from Union Station.

GUIDES and TOURS

The Chicago Office of Tourism operates Chicago Neighborhood Tours, with lengthy excursions to a different destination every Saturday (Tel. 312/742-1190). There are also private tour guides offering multilingual and individual services: AmeriTours (Tel. 773/792-2026), Chicago Tour Guides Institute, Inc. (Tel 773/276-6683), or Inlingua International Tours (Tel. 312/641-0488).

Architectural and sightseeing tours are also popular in Chicago. Information is available at the city's three Visitor's Information locations (see TOURIST INFORMATION OFFICES)

H

HEALTH and MEDICAL CARE

The US has the largest healthcare system in the world, and Chicago is arguably the capital of that system. It is home to the American Medical Association, the American Hospital Association, the American Dental Association, and the American College of Surgeons. Chicago is also an international center for academic medicine, with five universities offering degrees in health-related disciplines. There are 95 hospitals in the metropolitan area.

Hospitals and emergencies. If you need medical care at a hospital, call ahead to make specific arrangements. If you have a medical emergency, dial 911 on any public telephone (no coins needed), and an ambulance will take you to the nearest hospital.

Northwestern Memorial Hospital emergency room (Tel. 312/908-2000), at 233 East Superior Street, is arguably the best in the city; it is also near the Loop.

American hospitals are notorious for requiring medical insurance before admission. Foreign visitors are advised to purchase medical insurance for the duration of their visit. This can be arranged through an insurance company or through a travel agent.

Referrals to healthcare professionals can be obtained by phoning the following agencies:

Chicago Dental Association	(312) 836-7300
Medical Referral Service	(312) 670-2550
Physical Referral Service	(312) 908-8400
Medical Referral Service	(312) 670-2550

LANGUAGE

American English is spoken here, with a rather nasal accent heard most audibly in the vowels of native Midwesterners. Spanish, Polish, Chinese, Vietnamese, and other languages are spoken in the many immigrant communities.

Following is a brief glossary to prepare the international traveler for a few of the most common Anglo-American linguistic misunderstandings.

US	*British*
admission	entrance fee
bill	banknote
check	bill (restaurant)
collect call	reverse-charge call
dead end	cul-de-sac
detour	diversion
elevator	lift
faucet	tap
first floor	ground floor

gas(oline)	petrol
general delivery	poste restante
liquor	spirits
pants	trousers
purse/pocketbook	handbag
second floor	first floor
subway	underground
suspenders	braces
underpass/pedway	subway
undershirt	vest
vest	waistcoat

LAUNDRY and DRY CLEANING

Express laundry and dry cleaning services are available at most major hotels, but you will pay a high price. Neighborhood dry cleaners can generally provide next-day service. To see how the singles do it, take your own laundry to the Riverpoint Coin Laundry in Lincoln Park (1750 West Fullerton Avenue), a 24-hour coin Laundromat with an enormous fish tank and free coffee in the midnight hours; or tote your clothes up to the Saga Laundry Bar (3435 North Southport Avenue), where there's a sports bar and café on the premises along with the washing machines and soap dispensers.

M

MEDIA

In addition to its many radio and TV stations, wire services, and daily newspapers, Chicago is also home to over 60 ethnic newspapers and over 50 neighborhood newspapers that serve the city's diverse communities on a daily to monthly basis.

The two major daily newspapers, the *Chicago Tribune* and *Chicago Sun-Times*, are both morning papers. The *Tribune* is the largest newspaper in the Midwest, relatively conservative and read for business and world news as well as for local arts and entertainment. It has a good restaurant listing on Friday, with up-to-the-minute information on local eateries including what's hot and what's new. The *Sun-Times* is the city's tabloid. Befitting rival papers in a major city, both publications have great columnists who sometimes take swipes at one another. The papers naturally compete to scoop the city's breaking news.

Other significant papers are the *Daily Southtown* (serving the South Side) and the *Chicago Defender* (serving the city's African American community). Weekly publications of interest to tourists are the *Chicago Reader* and *New City*; both are free and have comprehensive listings of entertainment events and restaurants. Don't forget *Chicago* magazine, a monthly that is sold in many cities and airports nationwide.

Foreign-language newspapers can be found on the fourth floor of the Harold Washington Library (Tel. 312/542-7279).

And while Chicago has always been known as a great newspaper town, communication technology has expanded far beyond newsprint to include more than 100 metro area radio stations and 15 television stations. Chicago residents also have access to over 100 cable television stations.

Attending a TV show. The following shows are taped in Chicago and welcome visitors into their audiences. Admission is free, but call in advance for reservations.

Jenny Jones Show	Tel. (312) 836-9485
Jerry Springer Show	Tel. (312) 321-5365
Oprah Winfrey Show	Tel. (312) 591-9222

MONEY MATTERS

The unit of US currency is the dollar ($), divided into 100 cents (¢). Banknotes (bills) come in denominations of $1, $2, $5, $10, $20, $50, and $100.

Banks and currency exchange. Most offices called "currency exchanges" in Chicago are used by locals for cashing Illinois payroll checks and other simple transactions. It's generally easier to change foreign money at home or to travel with US traveler's checks in dollars. Traveler's checks in US dollars are accepted at most hotels, restaurants, and department stores, but the best place to cash a traveler's check is at a bank. Several foreign currency exchanges are: Chicago-LaSalle 24-hour Currency Exchange (777 North LaSalle Street; Tel. 312/642-0220), Rush Street Currency Exchange (12 East Walton Street; Tel. 312/337-7117), and World's Money Exchange, Inc. (6 East Randolph Street, Suite 204; Tel. 312/641-2151).

ATMs (Automated Teller Machines) dispense money on the street to applicable card holders or to holders of cards connected to their bank network.

Sales tax. A tax is added to almost everything you buy in Chicago. The basic sales tax is 8.75 percent, but some grocery and toiletries are taxed at only 2 percent. Quoted hotel and car rental rates *do not* include taxes; be prepared to see the taxes added to your final bill. Hotel tax: 14.9 percent; car rental tax: 18 percent. At restaurants, it is a generally accepted practice to tip on the pre-tax cost of the meal. Airport taxes are included in the cost of your airline ticket.

There is no value-added tax or other national tax in the US.

OPEN HOURS

Business hours are generally 8am to 5pm in Chicago. Government offices are open 8:30am to 4:30pm. Museum hours are generally 10am to around 4:30pm, but many are open late on select nights of the week or month. Many restaurants are open until at least 11pm. Final closing time for all bars and nightclubs is 5am, but most close around 3am or 4am.

POLICE

Officers of the Chicago Police Department patrol the streets of Chicago in marked and unmarked cars. To summon the police in an emergency, call 911. For non-emergency situations, call the police (Tel. 312/744-4000) or the fire department (Tel. 312/347-1313).

POST OFFICE

The US Postal Service deals only with mail. The main post office is downtown at 433 West Harrison Street, but there are numerous branches throughout the city; the telephone directory lists them all.

PUBLIC HOLIDAYS

In Chicago, as in other American cities, the following public holidays are usually observed with the closure of post offices, banks, government offices, and many museums. Some stores and restaurants might also close on these holidays; it is best to check in advance before making plans.

New Year's Day	1 January
Martin Luther King Day	third Monday in January
Presidents' Day	third Monday in February
Memorial Day	last Monday in May
Independence Day	4 July
Labor Day	first Monday in September
Columbus Day	second Monday in October
Veterans' Day	11 November
Thanksgiving Day	fourth Thursday in November
Christmas Day	25 December

PUBLIC TRANSPORTATION

CTA (Chicago Transit Authority). The CTA operates buses and elevated/subway trains (the "El") throughout the city and nearby suburbs. Public transportation is quite dependable and reliable; it will generally get you within walking distance of any metropolitan destination.

The "El" (elevated and subway trains) run on six lines identified by color and branch name (see map on cover flap); all lines converge downtown in the Loop. There are dozens of bus lines running on most major thoroughfares in the city. CTA buses stop about every 2 blocks at marked signs. Buses are marked with identifying signs in the front windshield. Signs list route number, route name, and destination.

Buses run every 10–15 minutes from before dawn until roughly 10 pm daily. Most routes are wheelchair accessible. Trains run daily every 5–15 minutes, pre-dawn to late evening. Customer assistants and security guards are available at most train stations to sell fare cards or admit riders paying cash fares.

CTA standard fare is $1.50; children aged 7 through 11 and senior citizens pay reduced fare of $0.75. Exact fare is required on buses and at "El" station turnstiles where there is no attendant present. Many "El" stations have automated machines selling farecards (often at a discount for multiple rides), with change provided for larger bills. Connections between CTA train lines are free; no transfer card is needed. If you are planning to transfer on the bus line, request a transfer when boarding. A transfer ticket, which costs $0.30 and can be used twice, is necessary when transferring between buses, or when transferring between the train and the bus system.

CTA Visitor Passes, offering unlimited use of CTA transportation, can be purchased at airports, train stations, hotels, visitor's centers, and various other locations. The current cost is $5 for a 1-day pass, $9 for a 2-day pass, $12 for a 3-day pass, $18 for a 5-day pass. The pass is a card that is inserted into the bus/train farecard machines; the card keeps track of how many days and rides you have taken.

CTA information: Tel. (312) 836-7000; TTY (312) 432-7139. General public transportation information: Tel. (312) 836-7000.

Taxis. Taxicabs can be hailed in most parts of town 24 hours a day, 365 days a year. Any driver must provide service to you unless the "Not for Hire" sign is clearly displayed in advance. Here is some important information about using a Chicago taxi:

Standard fare is charged in regulated cabs: $1.50 when you enter the cab, and $1.20 for each additional mile. There is a $0.50 charge for each additional passenger. It is customary to tip a cab driver 10 to 15 percent of the fare.

Cabs licensed with the City of Chicago may transport passengers from Chicago to anywhere within the city limits or suburbs. However, it is against the law for a suburban cab to transport passengers from one city location to another. Suburban cabs operating at Chicago's airports may take passengers into the suburbs only on prearranged trips.

At O'Hare and Midway Airports, an employee of the Department of Aviation called a "starter" is available in case of questions or problems in finding a taxi. Easily identifiable by a city ID, the starter will help arrange for your ride.

To prearrange a trip, call any one of the hundreds of taxicab companies operating in Chicago. For two of the biggest companies, try Checker Taxi Association (Tel. 312/243-2537) or Yellow Cab Company (Tel. 312/829-4222).

Limousines. Business travelers and families sometimes prefer to use a limousine rather than a taxi, particularly for trips to and from the airport or to major events. Fares vary, and there are circumstances when it is more affordable for a group to call a limousine: Amm's Limousine Service (Tel. 773/792-1126); B&B Limousine (Tel. 773/285-5466); BostonCoach (Tel. 312/444-2029); Carey Limousine Service (Tel. 312/663-1220); Chicago Flag Luxury Sedans and Limo/Tours/Shuttle (Tel. 312/944-4476); Chicago Limousine Service (Tel. 312/726-1035); Lake Point Limousines (Tel. 312/902-0526); Mahogany Limousine Service (Tel. 773/784-2121); and O'Hare Midway Limousine Service (Tel. 312/558-1111).

Access for disabled travelers. While some CTA buses are equipped with wheelchair lifts, the "El" lines are predominantly inaccessible to wheelchairs. Check with the Mayor's Office for People with Disabilities (Tel. 312/744-6673; TTY 312/744-7833).

R

RELIGION

Chicago's residents belong to every imaginable religious denomination. You will very likely find an appropriate house of worship, with services available in many languages. The Visitor Information Centers (see page 127) can provide you with listings.

T

TELEPHONE

The US telephone system is run by private regional companies. In Chicago, coin- or card-operated phones are found in all public places, and a local call can be made for a $0.35 coin deposit. Credit cards and phonecards can be used to make calls from specially marked telephone booths. Directions for use are clearly stated on the machine.

There are several area codes (three-digit prefixes) in the Chicago metropolitan area. For the Loop, the area code is 312. Outside the Loop in the city of Chicago, the area code is 773. Suburban area codes include 630, 708, and 847.

When dialing a number with an area code that differs from the phone you are using at the moment, you must dial 1 + the three-digit-area code + the seven-digit telephone number. When calling within the same area code, the seven-digit number is sufficient. The code 800 indicates a toll-free call.

For local directory assistance within the city of Chicago, dial 411. To obtain a telephone number anywhere in the US, dial the proper area code plus 555-1212. For a phone number in the suburb of Evanston, for example, you will dial 708-555-1212. Directory assistance can give you telephone numbers as well as street addresses.

Calling from hotels. Hotels generally charge a hefty fee for the use of in-room telephones (even for calling-card calls); it's better to know what you're paying than to be hit with an outrageous surcharge when you check out. Ask when you check in at the front desk. In most hotels, it is far cheaper to make local calls from a pay phone in the lobby.

If you have an American telephone calling card, by all means use it to make calls from your hotel. Prepaid calling cards for the area also can be purchased at convenience stores and at some hotels. The cards can save you time and money.

Information for the hearing-impaired. Telephone systems/numbers for hearing-impaired callers are universally indicated by the letters "TTY" preceding the listing. The city operates a 24-hour hotline for the hearing impaired (TTY 312/744-8599).

TICKETS for EVENTS

Tickets to all shows, concerts, and sporting events can be purchased at the individual box office or by calling the appropriate box office directly (see page 80). Tickets can also be purchased by phone via Ticketmaster (Tel. 312/559-1212). You will pay a service charge for using this outlet.

Hot Tix is the city's half-price, day-of-performance ticket outlet, mostly for theater and concerts. You must purchase in person (Tel. 312/977-1755 for hours and locations of Hot Tix Centers, or Tel. 900-225-2225 for a list of shows currently available).

TIME ZONES

The continental US is divided into four time zones. Chicago is in the Central Time Zone, on Central Standard Time (CST), which is 6 hours behind GMT. From April until October, the clock is advanced 1 hour for Central Daylight Time (GMT minus 5 hours). The following chart shows times in various cities in winter:

San Francisco	**Chicago**	New York	London	Sydney
10am	**noon**	1pm	6pm	5am (next day)

Note that Americans customarily write dates in the month/day/year order. Thus, in the US 12/5/99 means 5 December 1999.

TIPPING

You are expected to add a "tip" of at least 15 percent when paying restaurant bills, based on the total bill before taxes; you leave the tip on the table or add it to the credit card slip. Taxi drivers also expect tips. For exceptional service, 20 percent is appropriate. Doormen, cloakroom attendants, and housekeeping personnel at the hotel all should be given something (at least $0.50) at the time a service is performed. Additionally, it is customary to leave at least $5 or more in your room for the chambermaid, upon checkout. Bartenders are more attentive when tipped generously after each round of drinks (at least $1 per round is courtesy), and bathroom attendants in swanky restaurants or clubs who hand you a towel or turn on the water for you are expecting something as well.

TOURIST INFORMATION OFFICES

To call ahead for a free visitors' packet, and for help with accommodations, transportation, or general travel questions, call the Chicago Office of Tourism (Tel. 312/744-2400, 800-2CONNECT, toll-free; TTY 312/744-2947 or 800-406-6418, toll-free). The Office of Tourism maintains an extensive website at <www.ci.chi.il.us/Tourism>. You can also contact the Illinois Bureau of Tourism (Tel. 312/814-4732, 800-226-6632, toll-free).

The Chicago Office of Tourism has three visitor information locations where you can stop in for a wealth of information: Chicago Cultural Center (77 East Randolph Street; Tel. 312/744-2400; open 10am to 6pm daily); Chicago Water Works on North Michigan Avenue at Pearson Street, across from the Water Tower (Tel. 312/744-8783; open 7:30am to 7pm); Illinois Market Place Visitor Information Center on Navy Pier (Tel. 312/832-0010).

Information on the Internet. Many visitor services for Chicago can be accessed via the Internet, including general tourist information as well as rates and hours at specific attractions. A partial list includes:

Chicago Office of Tourism (information):
<www.ci.chi.il.us/Tourism>

Chicago Tribune (events and attractions):
<www.chicago.digitalcity.com>

Chicago Tribune (news): <www.chicago.tribune.com>

Chicago Reader (the city's free weekly newspaper):
<www.chireader.com>

Chicago

Hotels/accommodations:
<www.chicago.il.org/visitorinfo/accommodations>

Chicago Transit Authority: <www.transitchicago.com>

In addition, many of the city's cultural, business, and sporting attractions have websites that can be linked to through the Office of Tourism website.

WEIGHTS and MEASURES

Except for scientific and research purposes, the US does not use the international system of units for general measurements. Instead, on maps and most signage in the country, everything is listed in inches, feet, yards, miles, pounds, gallons, and degrees Fahrenheit.

Some useful equivalents: 1 US gallon=0.833 British imperial gallon=3.8 liters; 1 US quart=0.833 British imperial quart=0.9 liter; 1 mile=1.6 kilometers; 1 foot=30.48 centimeters; 1 acre=.4 hectares.

YOUTH HOSTELS

There are five youth hostels providing budget accommodations in the city. Valid youth hostel identification cards are generally required at the following: Three Arts Club of Chicago (300 North Dearborn Parkway; Tel. 312/944-6250; fax 312/944-6284); International House, at the University of Chicago (1414 East 59th Street; Tel. 773/753-2270; fax 773/753-1227); Chicago International Hostel (6318 North Winthrop Avenue; Tel. 773/262-1011; fax 773/262-3673); Hostelling International Chicago Summer Hostel (731 South Plymouth Court; Tel. 312/327-5350; fax 312/327-4287); Arlington House International Hostel (616 West Arlington Place; Tel. 312/929-5380, 800-467-8355, toll-free; fax 312/665-5485).

Recommended Hotels

There are more than 25,000 rooms for visitors in Chicago, from five-star hotels to youth hostels. Chicago's popularity for business meetings and major conventions can make room reservations a competitive sport. Book your room far in advance if you're planning a trip in mid-August, mid-October, or late November, as these are roughly the dates for the city's biggest conventions.

Following is an annotated selection of local accommodations, from luxury hotels to affordable motor lodges. Chicago has become a popular market for midsized hotels that offer full-service amenities in an intimate atmosphere.

In addition, Chicago has five youth hostels providing budget accommodations in the city (see page 128).

The Illinois Bureau of Tourism (Tel. 800-2CONNECT, toll-free) is very helpful for accommodation recommendations. You can also call the Illinois Reservation Service (Tel. 800-491-1800, toll-free) for assistance.

The price categories below are based on the lowest available daily rate for a standard room. Most hotels have suites that cost double and triple the price of a standard room. Many hotels offer midweek packages, winter holiday specials, and packages that include tickets to a cultural event.

✿✿✿✿✿	over $200
✿✿✿✿	$160–$200
✿✿✿	$120–$160
✿✿	$90–$120
✿	under $90

The Loop and Environs

Hotel Allegro ✿✿✿ *171 West Randolph Street; Tel. (312) 236-0123, 800-643-1500 (toll-free); fax (312) 236-3440.* The rooms are newly decorated in whimsical style and unusual colors. Fun, refreshing atmosphere in the city's downtown theater district; attached to world-renowned Palace Theater. Wheelchair access. 483 rooms. Major credit cards.

Blackstone Hotel ❀❀❀ *636 South Michigan Avenue; Tel. (312) 427-4300, 800-622-6330 (toll-free); fax (312) 427-4736.* Architectural landmark hotel built in 1910 is a little south of the action but still within walking distance of many Loop attractions. Many rooms have views of Grant Park and Lake Michigan. Wheelchair access. 305 rooms. Major credit cards.

Chicago Hilton and Towers ❀❀❀ *720 South Michigan Ave; Tel. (312) 922-4400, 800-445-8667 (toll-free); fax (312) 922-5240.* Overlooking Grant Park, this enormous hotel with luxury guest rooms, grand ballroom, health club, and indoor pool is a little out of the way, but makes up for it with attention to detail. Wheelchair access. 1,543 rooms. Major credit cards.

Fairmont Hotel Chicago ❀❀❀❀ *200 North Columbus Drive; Tel. (312) 565-8000, 800-527-4727 (toll-free); fax (312) 856-9020.* A luxury hotel with richly decorated rooms and spectacular views in a 45-story granite building near Grant Park, overlooking Lake Michigan and close to museums. Wheelchair access. 692 rooms. Major credit cards.

Hyatt on Printers' Row ❀❀❀ *500 South Dearborn Parkway; Tel. (312) 986-1234, 800-233-1234 (toll-free); fax (312) 939-2468.* Intimate and luxurious yet not far from many downtown attractions, with Prairie, one of the city's best restaurants, on the premises. Wheelchair access. 161 rooms. Major credit cards.

Hyatt Regency Chicago ❀❀❀ *151 East Wacker Drive; Tel (312) 565-1234, 800-233-1234 (toll-free); fax (312) 565-2648.* Enter one of the world's largest luxury convention hotels through the 3-story atrium lobby, with its reflecting pool and fountains. On the Chicago River, with six restaurants and cafés, close to all downtown destinations. Wheelchair access. 2,019 rooms. Major credit cards.

Hotel Monaco ✿✿✿✿ *224 North Wabash Avenue; Tel. (312) 960-8500, 800-397-7661 (toll-free); fax (312) 960-1883.* Young management makes the service in this beautiful new hotel near the river and Michigan Avenue a bit undependable, but the comfortable rooms are lively in décor. Wheelchair access. 192 rooms. Major credit cards.

Palmer House Hilton ✿✿✿ *17 East Monroe Street; Tel (312) 726-7500, 800-HILTONS (toll-free); fax (312) 263-2556.* The oldest continuously operating hotel in the US, this is a huge but lovely place with large, understated rooms. Set in the middle of the Loop, with a multilingual staff that speaks more than 30 languages. Fitness club includes golf simulator. Wheelchair access. 1,639 rooms. Major credit cards.

Renaissance Chicago Hotel ✿✿✿✿ *One West Wacker Drive; Tel. (312) 372-7200, 800-468-3571 (toll-free); fax (312) 372-0834.* One of the city's most upscale hotels, this 27-story tower filled with tasteful rooms is popular with business travelers because of its central location on the river, proximity to the Loop, and impersonal but impeccable atmosphere. Health club with indoor pool. Wheelchair access. 553 rooms. Major credit cards.

Swissotel Chicago ✿✿✿ *323 East Wacker Drive; Tel. (312) 565-0565, 800-637-9477 (toll-free); fax (312) 565-0540.* Overlooking the lake and the river, this is one of the city's newest luxury hotels. Rooms have great views, lovely contemporary furnishings, and amenities for business travelers. Skytop fitness center with pool. Wheelchair access. 630 rooms. Major credit cards.

North Michigan Avenue, River North, Gold Coast

Best Western Inn of Chicago ✿✿ *162 East Ohio Street; Tel (312) 787-3100, 800-557-BEST (toll-free); fax (312) 573-3136.* A great value near the Gold Coast and Michigan Avenue shopping. Basic but clean rooms; parking facilities. Wheelchair access. 357 rooms. Major credit cards.

Best Western River North Hotel ✿✿ *125 West Ohio Street; Tel. (312) 467-0800, 800-727-0800 (toll-free); fax (312) 467-1665.* A great bargain right in the middle of the Gold Coast nightlife scene. Basic décor and clean rooms, some overlooking the 24-hour Rock 'n' Roll McDonald's. Free parking, indoor pool, health club, sauna, sundeck. 146 rooms. Major credit cards.

Chicago Marriott Downtown ✿✿✿✿ *540 North Michigan Avenue; Tel. (312) 836-0100, 800-228-9290 (toll-free); fax (312) 245-6929.* This luxury hotel in a 46-story tower on the Magnificent Mile has impersonal rooms that are loaded with every amenity. Close to all downtown attractions; some rooms offer spectacular views. Expansive health club with indoor pool. Wheelchair access. 1,172 rooms. Major credit cards.

Doubletree Guest Suites ✿✿✿✿✿ *198 East Delaware Place; Tel. (312) 664-1100, 800-222-8733 (toll-free); fax (312) 664-8627.* A charming upscale facility that can feel almost like home, only a block from the Magnificent Mile. Every suite features a living room, bedroom, and bath. Rooftop health club with indoor pool, sauna, and whirlpool. Wheelchair access. 345 rooms. Major credit cards.

Drake Hotel ✿✿✿✿✿ *140 East Walton Place; Tel. (312) 787-2200, 800-553-7253 (toll-free); fax (312) 787-6324.* A landmark hotel listed on the US National Register of Historic Places. Prime location overlooking Lake Shore Drive and Oak Street beach on the Gold Coast at the tip of the Magnificent Mile. Rooms are subdued and newly renovated. Afternoon tea in the Palm Court is a lovely, regal experience. Fitness center. Wheelchair access. 535 rooms. Major credit cards.

Embassy Suites Hotel ✿✿✿✿ *600 North State Street; Tel. (312) 943-3800, 800-362-2779 (toll-free); fax (312) 943-7629.*

All-suite hotel on State Street between Ohio and Ontario, just steps from River North nightlife. Separate living room and bedroom in every suite. Built around an indoor atrium, this is a relatively noisy place. Indoor swimming pool, exercise facilities. Wheelchair access. 358 rooms. Major credit cards.

Four Seasons Hotel ✺✺✺✺✺ *120 East Delaware Place; Tel. (312) 280-8800, 800-332-3442 (toll-free); fax (312) 280-9184.* A celebrity favorite situated above the shops at 900 North Michigan Avenue, this is one of the city's premier hotels. Rooms are decorated with marble and handcrafted woodwork; many have fabulous views of the lake and city. Extensive health club, pool, sundeck. Wheelchair access. 343 rooms. Major credit cards.

Holiday Inn Chicago City Centre ✺✺✺✺ *300 East Ohio Street; Tel. (312) 787-6100, 800-465-4329 (toll-free); fax (312) 787-6259.* Excellent choice for business travelers or families, close to Michigan Avenue and Navy Pier, connected to McClurg Court Sports Center by indoor passage. Rooms have great views. Outdoor swimming pool available during summer months. Wheelchair access. 500 rooms. Major credit cards.

Hotel Inter-Continental Chicago ✺✺✺✺✺ *505 North Michigan Avenue; Tel. (312) 944-4100, 800-327-0200 (toll-free); fax (312) 944-3882.* Bustling Magnificent Mile location. Many rooms with lovely décor in this 1929 building included on the National Register of Historic Places. Junior Olympic-sized pool in spectacular health club. Wheelchair access. 844 rooms. Major credit cards.

House of Blues Hotel ✺✺✺✺ *333 North Dearborn Avenue; Tel. (312) 245-0333, 800-235-6397 (toll-free); fax (312) 923-2444.* A new hotel with dramatic lobby and rooms decorated in Gothic/New Orleans style. Close to River North night life, adjacent to House of Blues nightclub. Wheelchair access. 367 rooms. Major credit cards.

Ohio House Motel ❁ *600 North LaSalle Street; Tel. (312) 943-6000; fax (312) 943-6063.* Maybe the best bargain south of Oak Street, in the heart of River North nightlife. Rooms are comfortable and clean. Free parking. 50 rooms. Major credit cards.

Omni Ambassador East ❁❁❁❁ *301 North State Parkway; Tel. (312) 787-7200, 800-843-6664 (toll-free); fax (312) 787-9757.* Carefully restored to capture the rich style of Chicago in the 1920s, this lovely hotel in the Gold Coast has some very spacious rooms. Small fitness center. 275 rooms. Major credit cards.

Radisson Hotel and Suites ❁❁❁ *160 East Huron Street; Tel. (312) 787-2900, 800-346-2591 (toll-free); fax (312) 787-5158.* A high-rise hotel featuring spacious rooms, many with wonderful views of the city. Outdoor pool, health club, parking. Wheelchair access. 341 rooms. Major credit cards.

Raphael Hotel ❁❁❁ *201 East Delaware Place; Tel. (312) 943-5000, 800-983-7870 (toll-free); fax (312) 943-9483.* Small, popular, intimate hotel right near the Magnificent Mile. Spacious rooms with varying décor. Cocktail lounge with live entertainment. Wheelchair access. 172 rooms. Major credit cards.

Ritz-Carlton Chicago ❁❁❁❁❁ *160 East Pearson Street; Tel. (312) 266-1000, 800-621-6906 (toll-free); fax (312) 266-1194.* A Four Seasons Regent Hotel with a reputation for large, plush rooms, scrupulous service, and first-rate amenities that include an indoor pool and one of the best restaurants in the city, The Dining Room. Wheelchair access. 429 rooms. Major credit cards.

Sheraton Chicago Hotel and Towers ❁❁❁ *301 East North Water Street; Tel. (312) 464-1000, 800-233-4100 (toll-free); fax (312) 329-7045.* A new mega-hotel overlooking the river, with good-sized rooms, some with excellent views. Largest ballroom in the Midwest; full health club with indoor pool. Wheelchair access. 1,200 rooms. Major credit cards.

Talbott Hotel ✦✦✦✦✦ *20 East Delaware Place; Tel. (312) 944-4970, 800-621-8506 (toll-free); fax (312) 944-7241.* All the spacious rooms in this intimate and luxurious hotel (once an apartment building; located two blocks from Water Tower Place) have kitchen facilities. Wheelchair access. 147 rooms. Major credit cards.

Tremont Hotel ✦✦✦✦ *100 East Chestnut Street; Tel. (312) 751-1900, 800-621-8133 (toll-free); fax (312) 751-8691.* A renovated apartment building, this hotel has European elegance, intimacy, a cozy lobby with fireplace, bright sunny rooms, and most of the service amenities of a larger hotel. Wheelchair access. 129 rooms. Major credit cards.

Westin River North Chicago ✦✦✦✦✦ *320 North Dearborn Avenue; Tel. (312) 744-1900, 800-937-8461 (toll-free); fax (312) 527-2664.* International luxury hotel with Japanese touches. Rooms feature in-room fax machines and other business amenities. Fitness center with workout attire provided. Wheelchair access. 422 rooms. Major credit cards.

Whitehall Hotel ✦✦✦✦✦ *105 East Delaware; Tel. (312) 944-6300, 800-948-4255 (toll-free); fax (312) 573-6250.* Popular hotel close to Magnificent Mile, with traditional country-inn ambiance and lovely British décor. Exercise room. Wheelchair access. 221 rooms. Major credit cards.

Wyndham Ambassador West ✦✦✦✦ *1300 North State Parkway; Tel. (312) 787-3700, 800-300-WEST (toll-free); fax (312) 640-2967.* European-style hotel with wood-and-tapestry room décor is two blocks from Rush Street and just minutes from North Michigan Avenue, lakefront, and the beach. Wheelchair access. 219 rooms. Major credit cards.

The North Side

Belden-Stratford ✦✦ *2300 North Lincoln Park West; Tel. (773) 281-2900, 800-800-8301 (toll-free); fax (773) 880-2039.*

Chicago

This small but elegant hotel across from Lincoln Park Conservatory is an upscale apartment building that also makes available to guests some individually decorated suites (with kitchenettes) of various sizes and a wide price range. 25 rooms. Major credit cards.

City Suites Hotel ❋ *933 West Belmont Avenue; Tel. (773) 404-3400.* Excellent value in this clean, bright facility with Lakeview/Lincoln Park location, close to neighborhood nightlife and Wrigley Field and right near the "El." Operated by Neighborhood Inns of Chicago. Wheelchair access. 45 rooms. Major credit cards.

Comfort Inn Lincoln Park ❋ *601 West Diversey Parkway; Tel. (773) 348-2810, 800-228-5150 (toll-free); fax (312) 348-1912.* You're out of downtown but not far from the action, the Lincoln Park Zoo, and neighborhood watering holes. Motel with free parking and clean, comfortable rooms. Wheelchair access. 74 rooms. Major credit cards.

Days Inn Lincoln Park ❋ *644 West Diversey Parkway; Tel. (773) 525-7010, 888-576-3297 (toll-free); fax (773) 525-6998.* Old-World charm in newly renovated lobby and guest rooms. Offers special business-oriented rooms with spacious sitting areas equipped for laptops. Close to Lincoln Park Zoo, Wrigley Field, and Lake Michigan. Free health club passes. Wheelchair access. 130 rooms. Major credit cards.

Park Brompton Inn ❋❋ *528 West Brompton Street; Tel. (773) 404-3499, 800-727-5108 (toll-free); fax (773) 404-3495.* A quaint English-style inn located in a Lakeview residential neighborhood near Lake Michigan and Wrigley Field. Rooms have lovely 4-poster beds and tapestry furnishings. Operated by Neighborhood Inns of Chicago. 52 rooms. Major credit cards.

Recommended Restaurants

There are hundreds of restaurants in Chicago, featuring food from American to Ukrainian. With the exception of the city's most formal establishments, a nice pair of slacks and something a bit more than sneakers and a T-shirt will get you in the door. The following listing provides a representative sample of cuisines, prices, and city neighborhoods. Reservations are essential at some establishments, as indicated.

The price categories indicate the cost for a three-course meal for one person, excluding drinks, tax, and tip:

✿✿✿✿	over $35
✿✿✿	$25–$35
✿✿	$15–$25
✿	under $15

Loop and North Michigan Avenue

The Berghoff ✿✿ *17 West Adams Street; Tel. (312) 427-3170.* A Chicago landmark serving German and American food in the Loop since 1898. Try the stand-up bar for lunch. They even have their own brand of beer. Serving lunch and dinner daily except Sunday. Major credit cards.

Bistro 110 ✿✿✿ *110 East Pearson Street; Tel. (312) 266-3110.* Large, lively bistro two blocks from the Water Tower. French cuisine, with oven-roasted garlic chicken a specialty. Stylish crowd. Open daily for lunch and dinner. Major credit cards.

Brasserie Jo ✿ *59 West Hubbard Street; Tel. (312) 595-0800.* Authentic, affordable French food just a few blocks off Michigan Avenue. Dinner served daily; lunch Monday–Friday only. Reservations recommended. Major credit cards.

Chicago Chop House ✿✿✿ *60 West Ontario Street; Tel. (312) 787-7100.* Popular steak house in a restored Victorian brownstone serving massive portions. Piano bar. Dinner served daily; lunch Monday–Friday only. Major credit cards.

Cité ✹✹✹✹ *505 North Lake Shore Drive; Tel. (312) 644-4050.* On the 70th floor of prestigious residential towers overlooking the lake, this restaurant serves fine Continental cuisine with a first-class view. Dinner served daily; lunch Monday–Friday only; Sunday brunch. Major credit cards.

Everest ✹✹✹✹ *440 South LaSalle Street; Tel. (312) 663-8920.* Fine French cuisine served along with spectacular views on the 40th floor in the Chicago Stock Exchange building. Dinner only; closed Sunday and Monday. Major credit cards.

Heaven on Seven ✹ *111 North Wabash Avenue (7th floor); Tel. (312) 263-6443.* Great Cajun food and fun, festive atmosphere in this small, crowded daytime spot. Open for breakfast and lunch Monday–Saturday; dinner served on the first and third Friday of every month. No credit cards.

Mity Nice Grill ✹✹ *Water Tower Place (mezzanine level), 835 North Michigan Avenue; Tel. (312) 335-4745.* Walk through the mall's food court and find this hidden treasure that's just like home. Open daily for lunch and dinner. Major credit cards.

Nick's Fishmarket ✹✹✹✹ *One First National Plaza (79 West Monroe Street); Tel. (312) 621-0200.* Intimate seafood restaurant, highly popular for great food and attentive service. Piano bar. Dinner served daily except Sunday; lunch Monday–Friday only; reservations recommended. Major credit cards.

Morton's Of Chicago ✹✹✹✹ *1050 North State Street; Tel. (312) 266-4820.* Chicago's top-rated steak house, with a club-like setting. Open daily for dinner only; reservations recommended. Major credit cards.

Pizzeria Uno ✹ *29 East Ohio Street; Tel. (312) 321-1000.* The birthplace of Chicago deep-dish pizza. Open daily. Major credit cards.

Prairie ❀❀❀ *500 South Dearborn Street (in the Hyatt on Printer's Row); Tel. (312) 663-1143.* American cuisine in Frank Lloyd Wright-inspired setting in Printer's Row district. Open daily for lunch and dinner. Major credit cards.

Printer's Row ❀❀❀❀ *550 South Dearborn Street; Tel. (312) 461-0780.* First-class New American cuisine in cozy, elegant setting. Dinner served daily except Sunday; lunch served Monday–Friday only. Major credit cards.

Rhapsody ❀❀❀ *65 East Adams Street; Tel. (312) 786-9911.* Luxurious restaurant in Symphony Center, serving contemporary American cuisine and scrumptious desserts. Dinner served daily; lunch Monday–Friday only; reservations recommended. Major credit cards.

Ritz-Carlton Dining Room ❀❀❀❀ *160 East Pearson Street (12th floor), in the Ritz-Carlton Hotel; Tel. (312) 573-5223.* The city's highest-rated hotel restaurant serves inventive French cuisine in a plush, elegant setting. Open daily for dinner only; Sunday brunch; reservations strongly recommended. Major credit cards.

Riva ❀❀❀ *700 East Grand Avenue (on Navy Pier); Tel. (312) 644-7482.* Seafood and steakhouse with great views off Navy Pier. Open for lunch and dinner daily; reservations recommended. Major credit cards.

Rosebud On Rush ❀❀*720 North Rush Street; Tel. (312) 266-6444.* Newer downtown branch of popular Rosebud Café (in Little Italy), serving large portions of Italian comfort food. Dinner served daily; lunch Monday–Friday only. Major credit cards.

Russian Tea Time ❀❀ *77 East Adams Street; Tel. (312) 360-0000.* Serving robust Russian specialties, with a top location for Loop culture seekers (near Art Institute and Orchestra Hall). Open daily for lunch and dinner. Major credit cards.

Seasons ❀❀❀❀ *120 East Delaware Place (in the Four Seasons Hotel); Tel. (312) 649-2349.* Contemporary food in a sumptuous setting. This is a favorite place for special occasions. Open daily for breakfast, lunch, and dinner; reservations recommended. Major credit cards.

Shaw's Crab House and Blue Crab Lounge ❋❋ *21 East Hubbard Street; Tel. (312) 527-2722.* Bustling, informal atmosphere, with great shellfish; live music and dancing in lounge. Open daily for lunch and dinner. Major credit cards.

Signature Room at the 95th ❋❋❋ *875 North Michigan Avenue (in the John Hancock Center); Tel. (312) 787-9596.* The views from the 95th floor are splendid in this restaurant serving contemporary American cuisine. Open daily for lunch and dinner. Major credit cards.

Spiaggia ❋❋❋❋ *980 North Michigan Avenue (2nd floor); Tel. (312) 280-2750.* Excellent nouveau Italian food served in a duplex dining room with enchanting views. Dinner served daily; lunch Tuesday–Saturday only. Major credit cards.

West Loop and River North

Coco Pazzo ❋❋❋❋ *300 West Hubbard Street; Tel. (312) 836-0900.* Regional Italian cuisine in contemporary, refined setting, this is a current Chicago favorite. Dinner served daily; lunch Monday–Friday only. Major credit cards.

Ed Debevic's ❋ *640 North Wells Street; Tel. (312) 664-1707.* One of the original theme restaurants: a 1950s setting with homestyle food. Open daily for lunch and dinner. Major credit cards.

Frontera Grill ❋❋❋ *445 North Clark Street; Tel. (312) 661-1434.* Festive, popular "nuevo" Mexican food in the heart of River North neighborhood. Dinner served Tuesday–Saturday; lunch on Saturday only. Major credit cards.

Gene and Georgetti ❋❋❋ *500 North Franklin Street; Tel. (312) 527-3718.* Popular steakhouse for more than 50 years. Open Monday–Saturday for lunch and dinner. Major credit cards.

Gordon ❀❀❀❀ *500 North Clark Street; Tel. (312) 467-9780.* Romantic contemporary American restaurant with jazz and intimate dance floor in River North; this is one of the city's best. Dinner served daily; lunch Tuesday–Friday only; reservations recommended. Major credit cards.

Indian Garden Restaurant ❀❀ *247 East Ontario Street; Tel. (312) 280-4910.* Authentic Indian cuisine in this branch of a three-restaurant "chain"; another is on Devon Avenue on the North Side. Open daily for lunch and dinner. Major credit cards.

Marché ❀❀❀ *833 West Randolph Street; Tel. (312) 226-8399.* An ultra-hip French eclectic restaurant in a renovated loft setting. Loud and chic, with trendy West Loop crowd, interesting appetizers, wait staff with attitude, and a fun wine list. Dinner served daily; lunch Monday–Friday only. Major credit cards.

Scoozi! ❀❀❀ *410 West Huron Street; Tel. (312) 943-5900.* One of the lively "Lettuce Entertain You" establishments, serving nouveau Italian food in loft-like setting in the River North gallery district. Dinner served daily; lunch Monday–Friday only. Major credit cards.

Vivo ❀❀❀ *838 West Randolph Street; Tel. (312) 733-3379.* The original West Loop spot to "see and be seen," serving innovative Italian food. Dinner served daily; lunch Monday–Friday only. Major credit cards.

North Side

Ambria ❀❀❀❀ *2300 North Lincoln Park West; Tel. (773) 472-5959.* One of the city's finest restaurants, serving exquisite contemporary French cuisine in an Art Nouveau setting. This is where Chicagoans go for special occasions. Extensive wine list. Open Monday–Saturday for dinner only. Major credit cards.

Ann Sather's ❀ *939 West Belmont Avenue; Tel. (773) 348-2378; and 5207 North Clark Street; Tel. (773) 271-6677.* This informal, cozy restaurant featuring home-like Swedish food is a great place for brunch. Don't leave without trying the cinnamon rolls. Two locations serving breakfast, lunch, and dinner daily. Major credit cards.

Bangkok ✿✿ *3542 North Halsted Street; Tel. (773) 327-2870.* One of the best in a city known for its Thai food, with a very popular weekend brunch. Open daily for lunch and dinner. Major credit cards.

Blue Mesa ✿✿ *1729 North Halsted Street; Tel. (312) 944-5990.* This Southwestern charmer in Lincoln Park is popular for its blue chips, great margaritas, and lovely outdoor garden. Closed Monday, except during the summer. Major credit cards.

Le Bouchon ✿✿✿ *1958 North Damen Avenue; Tel. (773) 862-6600.* A crowded Bucktown bistro with a European atmosphere. Dinner only, served Monday–Saturday. Major credit cards.

Cafe Absinthe ✿✿ *1954 West North Avenue; Tel (773) 278-4488.* Funky, Bucktown must-see restaurant: enter from the alley, draw aside the curtains, order something "French eclectic." Open daily for dinner only. Major credit cards.

Café Ba-Ba-Reeba ✿✿ *2024 North Halsted Street; Tel. (773) 935-5000.* This bustling Spanish tapas bar in Lincoln Park is a great place to go with a crowd. Nice outdoor courtyard. Dinner served daily; lunch on Friday, Saturday, and Sunday only. Major credit cards.

Carson's: The Place For Ribs ✿✿ *612 North Wells Street; Tel. (312) 280-9200.* The city's original award-winning rib house, popular for takeout. Open daily for lunch and dinner. Major credit cards.

Charlie Trotter's ✿✿✿✿ *816 West Armitage Avenue; Tel. (773) 248-6228.* Outstanding restaurant in Old Town, with an international reputation for contemporary multicultural cuisine. Dinner only, served Tuesday–Saturday; reservations highly recommended. Major credit cards.

Deleece ❀ *4004 North Southport Avenue; Tel. (773) 325-1710.* Eclectic, fun, affordable contemporary California-influenced food in Southport, not far from Wrigley Field. Dinner served daily; brunch served on Sunday. Major credit cards.

Geja's Café ❀❀ *340 West Armitage Avenue; Tel. (773) 281-9101.* Romantic fondue restaurant in Old Town, featuring flamenco guitar music nightly. Dinner only, served daily. Major credit cards.

Indian Garden Restaurant ❀❀ *2548 West Devon Avenue; Tel. (773) 338-2929.* Experience the best of Chicago's Indian cuisine in the heart of the authentic Asian neighborhood on Devon Avenue (a branch of this restaurant is in River North). Open daily for lunch and dinner. Major credit cards.

Mia Francesca ❀❀ 3311 North Clark Street; Tel. (773) 281-3310. Sister restaurant to Francesca's on Taylor (in Little Italy), with generous servings of contemporary Italian fare. Open daily for lunch and dinner except Monday. Major credit cards.

Pasteur ❀❀ *5525 North Broadway; Tel. (773) 878-1061.* Fabulous Vietnamese cuisine with French influence. Dinner served daily; lunch Wednesday–Sunday only. Major credit cards.

Penny's Noodle Shop ❀ *950 West Diversey Parkway; Tel. (773) 281-8448; and 3400 North Sheffield Avenue; Tel. (773) 281-8222.* Outstanding Asian noodle shops; go at off-hours if you don't want to wait. Closed Monday. No credit cards.

Salpicon ❀❀❀ *1252 North Wells Street; Tel. (312) 988-7811.* Creative Mexican food in a lively Old Town setting. Dinner served daily; lunch on Sunday only. Major credit cards.

Soul Kitchen ❀❀ *1576 North Milwaukee Avenue; Tel. (773) 342-9742.* Bold, spicy Southern food and loud music in this Wicker Park hot spot. Dinner served daily; brunch on Sunday only. Major credit cards.

Chicago

Yoshi's Café ✿✿✿ *3257 North Halsted Street; Tel (773) 248-6160.* French-Japanese bistro serving innovative food with notable specialties and an internationally known chef. Dinner only, Tuesday–Sunday. Major credit cards.

Greektown, Little Italy, and Chinatown

Emperor's Choice ✿✿ *2238 South Wentworth Avenue; Tel. (312) 225-8800.* Low on décor but high on Cantonese specialties, especially seafood. A Chinatown favorite and well worth the trip. Open daily for lunch and dinner. Major credit cards.

Francesca's on Taylor ✿✿ *1400 West Taylor Street; Tel. (312) 829-2828.* Popular sister restaurant of Mia Francesca (on the North Side), serving huge portions of innovative Italian food. Open daily for lunch and dinner except Monday. Major credit cards.

Greek Islands ✿✿ *200 South Halsted Street; Tel. (312) 782-9855.* Lively Greektown location with an enormous dining room and friendly staff. Open daily for lunch and dinner. Major credit cards.

Parthenon ✿✿ *314 South Halsted Street; Tel. (312) 726-2407.* Greektown favorite and a good value. Open daily for lunch and dinner. Major credit cards.

Rosebud Café ✿✿ *1500 West Taylor Street; Tel. (312) 942-1117.* Quaint Italian restaurant in Little Italy for over 20 years. Huge portions, good food. Dinner served daily; lunch on Monday–Friday only. Major credit cards.

Northwest Suburbs

Le Français ✿✿✿✿ *10 miles (16 km) north of O'Hare Airport.* Le Français is consistently selected as Chicagoland's top restaurant and known nationwide for chef/owner Roland Liccioni's fine French cuisine. Open daily for dinner except Sunday; lunch Monday–Friday only; reservations highly recommended. Major credit cards.